Yours Truly,

John

Yours Truly, John

A Memoir

Joyce Stubblefield Pattillo

ISBN: 979-8-9879632-6-5

Front cover photograph by Jimmy Katz
Back cover illustration by John's son, John C. Stubblefield
Cover and book design by H. K. Stewart

Unless otherwise indicated, all photographs are from the Stubblefield family archives, the John Stubblefield Papers in the Special Collections Library at the University of Arkansas in Fayetteville, or courtesy of Jimmy Katz.

Printed in the United States of America

With gratitude to God, this book is affectionately dedicated to
our parents, **Johnnie C.** and **Mable Stubblefield**;
our brother, **William Stubblefield**;
John's granddaughter, **Halie Shae Stubblefield**,
embodying his spirit of entertainment;
and to my grandchildren, who fill my life with boundless joy.
With love, Nana J

Contents

Acknowledgments

The completion of this book marks a profound journey, initiated as I wrote its first pages on a flight from New York City to Little Rock after John's transition in July 2005. Although the book lingered in my heart for years, the words eluded me. I am filled with gratitude for all of the incredible individuals who played a crucial role in bringing this book to life.

Gratitude goes to **Barbara Bohannon** for sparking ideas for this book in 2006; **Aisha Credit** for introducing me to **Carolyn Hobbs**, an author who encouraged me to outline chapters and begin writing, and who facilitated the connection with my editor, **H. K. Stewart**. H. K., I am grateful for your composed demeanor, along with your insightful expertise and guidance. You illuminated my true mission for this book and led me step by step through the whole process. Again, my heartfelt thanks for your commitment and steadfast support.

To my son, **Conrad Pattillo**, for your encouragement and inspiration to capture the full essence of John's life. And to our aunt **Irea Stubblefield**, John's cheerleader, who transitioned at 98 in 2021—your presence resonates. Gratitude extends to cousins **Harry Veronica Stubblefield** and **Stephanie Barber** for their enduring love and encouragement.

Deborah Johnston and **Bea Klokpah**, thank you for your untiring support in keeping me on track throughout the writing of this book. **Sean West**, your exceptional talent and artistic contributions are deeply appreciated. And **Zach Kirsimae**, you were the glue that held *everything* together, from organizing concerts, coordinating interviews, to scheduling, texting, and tirelessly compiling contact lists. Many thanks, Zach; I couldn't have done it without you!

Special appreciation to **Henry Linton** and the Museum and Cultural Center staff at the University of Arkansas at Pine Bluff and to the Special Collections Libraries of the University of Arkansas at Fayetteville—**Adam Helen**, **Chris Galindo**, and **Rebekah Mason**. Access to the John Stubblefield papers is available through this website: https://libraries.uark.edu/Special Collections or by contacting the University of Arkansas Libraries.

Finally, I extend heartfelt gratitude to **Sue Mingus**, who passed away in September 2022, and to the **Mingus Band Family**. Sue's unwavering support remains eternally cherished, and her absence is deeply felt. To the rest of the Mingus Band Family your steadfast presence during difficult moments resonates profoundly, and for that, I am forever grateful.

Prelude

Hello, I am Joyce Stubblefield Pattillo, often known as John Stubblefield's Little Sister. I invite you to delve into the pages of this book with the hope that each reader will gain profound insights into John's life. Throughout this book, the focus is portraying my brother as an artful, professional musician deeply immersed and captivated by every facet of "The Music."

John Stubblefield stands as one of the most highly respected jazz saxophonists of his generation, leaving an indelible mark through his collaborations with legendary musicians. Over three decades, he crafted a legacy as a composer, writer arranger, bandleader, and sought-after studio and live performer. Although John has transitioned, his life echoes through his music and the lives he touched. This book aims to reveal the essence of who John was, encouraging readers to cherish the memories that persist beyond his physical presence. May this book vividly portray his life, passion, and genius for "The Music" and help you envision "Yours Truly, John" as you explore these pages. Enjoy the journey.

I. Early Years

Our parents' love story began in December 1943 at a Christmas dinner set up by Dad's brother and sister-in-law, Willie and Irea Stubblefield. Mom, visiting from Tuckerman, Arkansas, caught Dad's attention, and the rest unfolded as a charming story frequently told by our father. Dad, always ready to offer Mom a ride back home, playfully recounted Mom's responses about the weather whenever he suggested taking her home. Ultimately, Mom never returned to Tuckerman, and they were married on January 19, 1944. Their journey continued, and when baby John was just six weeks old, Mom and Dad bought our family home at 3105 Chester Street. It was a modest house in the Southend of Little Rock. This home would become the backdrop for countless family memories and the early chapters of John's remarkable life.

Dad and Mom welcomed John on February 4, 1945. John's baby book has been kept all these years and was a perfect source for first-hand information regarding the first years of his life. Mom and Dad recorded the following things about John. Johnnie Stubblefield (AKA John Stubblefield) was born to Mable and Johnnie Cornelius Stubblefield at 1:50 a.m. at the Lena Jordan Hospital in Little Rock, Arkansas.

As an aside, John often shared with me the rich history of the hospital, which was established in 1932 by Lena Lowe Jordan, an African American pioneer. He frequently emphasized the historical significance of the hospital, founded by an African American woman, where both he and our brother William came into the world.

According to an article written by Chris Hughes in the Arkansas Medical History files at the Central Arkansas Library System, Lena Lowe Jordan, the founder of the hospital, was a registered nurse. The hospital provided surgical, medical, and obstetrical care for African American patients, as well as nurse training. It also offered care for physically disabled black children. Nurse Jordan's vision for healthcare for African Americans was far-reaching and provided general healthcare for many people. Although the hospital ceased operations in 1953, the city repurposed the facility, and the Dunbar Community Center was opened in that location in 1954. The Lena Jordan Hospital, where John began his journey into the world, held a special place in his life. Today as a community center, it continues to play a vital role in the African American community. While growing up, John experienced sports, Boy Scouts, school musicals, many jam sessions, and other performances at the Dunbar Community Center.

Getting back to John's early years, his weight was seven pounds, five ounces according to his recorded birth certificate #1901. Mom wrote John had brown eyes, black hair, and a beautiful brown complexion. His first visitor was a neighbor, Mrs. Ward, grandmother of my dear friend Edward Evans, better known as "Chief."

Gifts for his arrival included his baby book, clothing, blankets, and a bonnie set. It is also recorded that he recognized his mouth at two months, sat up at four months, recognized his hands at five months, cut his first teeth at eight months (four), pulled up and crawled at nine months, and walked at 11 months. His first words were "Da Da." John celebrated his first Christmas with gifts and visits from aunts and uncles. John's first birthday was a big celebration with a cake baked by our mom. Gifts included a suit, a pair of creepers, and $2.25. He received his first haircut on March 6, 1946, given by our dad while John was sitting on the vanity stool by the bed. Daddy jokingly commented in the book, "Before the haircut, he looked like a bear and after a monkey." Dad was always full of jokes.

Mom also recorded in this book that she prayed with John, "Lord, I lay me down to sleep. I pray the Lord my soul to keep. If I should die before I wake, I pray the Lord my soul to take— Amen." By the age of two he was able to repeat the prayer alone. This would remain the family home until the property was purchased as part of urban renewal in 1969. This is the house where John grew up and where his love for music began.

Family Life

After John's birth, our family continued to expand with the arrival of our brother William Lynatte Stubblefield in November 1946 and myself in April 1951. Our parents and our shared family life set the stage for John's formative years and helped lay the path for his immersion in "The Music."

Despite challenges in completing their formal education, our parents' self-taught wisdom and practical skills greatly influenced our upbringing. Dad's craftsmanship and Mom's nurturing focus established a sturdy ground work for our education and essential life skills. Their teachings, grounded in faith, prioritized the three R's and fundamental life skills equipping us for successful and responsible adulthood.

Mom and Dad served as our initial mentors, imparting invaluable principles that formed the bedrock of our educational journey. From our earliest years, they instilled in us a deep respect for God and the practice of prayer, emphasizing spirituality's significance. Their affection and commitment permeated every aspect of our lives. Through unfaltering support and effective home teachings, our parents became our primary educators, laying the foundation for our spiritual, academic, and personal growth. As we entered public school, we did so with assurance and preparedness.

I am profoundly thankful for our parent's love and holistic approach to raising us. Their teachings were reinforced through repetition and exceptional home guidance, ensuring we acquired crucial life skills essential for our journey into responsible adulthood.

Back to Dad's inventions, they were numerous—you name it, he could make it work. His inventions were always items that made things more convenient at home and at work. He had a well-organized workshop in the basement of our home where he worked for hours on his projects. In this workshop you would find his special work bench, vices, and all types of tools, and I remember the buzzing sound of the grinder. John and William would spend time with him in the workshop learning the basics; however, this was not their true passion. We also never had any concern about our car breaking down because if it did, there was no doubt Dad would fix it in quickly.

Another memory is when Dad decided he was going to dig out the entire basement and build a room. To do this, he hired a contractor named Moncrief. I recall that name because when Moncrief was going down the wrong path during this project, Dad would bellow his name out loud and get him on the phone and get him back on track. Dad decided the new room would be in the basement adjacent to his workshop. Based on the location of this room, the only way to access the room would be from the front porch. So, imagine this—he had a trap door the size of a regular door placed on the porch. On each end of the trap door, there were locks that had to be opened to get into the room. He had the front porch reconstructed in concrete, and the door was framed at the back of the porch. When the door was opened, there were narrow steps (burnt orange in color) that led straight down into the room.

This was the new bedroom that was given to John. It had everything—full bed, easy chair, TV, and a black wall phone that I spent many hours talking on. While my dad was happy about his completed project, our mom was not because she wanted the new room added to the outside of the house.

I tell this story because of a trip I made to Disney World in 1986. On the way, I stopped in Mobile, Alabama, and toured the USS Alabama Battleship. During the tour, I had a flash back regarding our basement bedroom! Having been in the Navy, Dad had based this room on his ship. As I walked along, I saw the same burnt orange narrow steps, and the trap door represented the many overhead doors we traveled through during the tour. I could not believe it, but it was true. Dad had recreated a piece of his Navy experience in our home. Eventually, Dad did build that outside room for Mom.

While growing up, if we got a cold, we were not sick for long. I remember Dad would tell us about how his parents would go outside and get cow chips and make tea for them to drink to get well. Of course, we found this to be awful, and we would tell him we were glad we did not live back then in the "old days." Dad would just respond, "We got well." Anyway, with any signs of a cold, we knew the ritual Dad had for us. First, he would cut up fresh lemons and make a lemon tea. In that tea he would put honey, and we would have to drink it and get into the bed and sweat the cold out. If the cold was lingering, he would boil water and place a towel over the pot. As the steam rose, he would put Vicks VapoRub on the center of the towel and safely hold us as we inhaled the steam. "We got well." During the winter, another ritual was that we'd have to line up before we left the house for school to take a spoonful of cod liver oil. As I look back, it was truly nasty, but we were seldom ill because Mom and Dad were always there taking the best of care of us.

Our dad was always there for us—thinking and developing new things and this is a similar trait found in John while growing up. John was a deep thinker, and like our dad he focused on the music with the same intensity. Dad purchased our first TV in the early 50s around the time John began piano lessons. I remember this TV was made by Zenith and it was a three-in-one—TV, radio, and record player. This TV brought both an audible and visual experience into our home. We all enjoyed the entertainment; however, John was fascinated with watching the Liberace show, weekly variety shows, and the performance of the Big Bands. This was a great influence on John around the age of 11 or 12. Dad was a Big Band fan; he would tell us about the bands he had heard. He told us he loved music and spent hours on the floor dancing to that music played by the masters John would later study. John loved to hear these stories. It was a hand-and-glove fit for John's future goal to be a musician. John would often use a statement he remembered from Louis Armstrong: "All great musicians have to come to New York." That statement remained with John, and he looked forward to one day moving in New York and playing "the Music."

Again, because Dad invented different things, the kids in the neighborhood would call him the "crazy inventor," and because he was a mechanic, they called him the "grease monkey." As children growing up, we did not like for these things to be said about our dad; however, in later years John and I concluded, it was actually a compliment.

As adults John and I would reminisce about a few other things regarding our dad. Growing up, we loved when Dad would take us to War Memorial Park where we spent time at the zoo and amusement park. We would stroll through the zoo looking at all the animals and then off to the rides (e.g., carousel, tilt-a world, bumper cars, etc.). There was Rosie, the laughing lady in front of the Ghost House who greeted us with her deep guttural laugh. Inside this house, it was dark, and as we rolled around, things would pop out at us, and of course there were many ghostly sounds. We had the best time with Dad and Mom on our trips to War Memorial Park on Sundays. In addition to the zoo and rides, there were games, food, cotton candy, and chances to win lots of stuff. We really looked forward to these trips.

A final memory of Dad was his teaching phrases. He had a way of challenging us to think about things we wanted to do and what the results might bring. If he had given his advice and we were still wanting it our way, he would say, "It's your red wagon. You can push it, pull it, or go-cart it." It took years, but we finally figured it out. If we were misbehaving and Dad felt we did not get the point, his famous words were, "I guess you do not believe fat meat is greasy." Of course, it is, and the other part of his statement to us was, "Then you had better straighten up and fly right." I promise he had excellent hearing. If we were talking back to Mom, he could hear it and would say from the other room, "What did you say?" and that was the end of it. We did not want to see him come into the room. Actually, he did not have to. His voice was enough. As we got older and really tried to push the card with him, he would just look at us and calmly say, "Keep living." This was a powerful statement. He was definitely right, and as adults we came to know and understand exactly what he meant by this. When we were obsessing over something, his saying to us was, "You gag at a gnat and swallow a camel."It really took a while to absorb this one. As children and adults, we did tend to focus on minor issues while neglecting more significant matters. Our dad taught by example; John picked up Dad's ability to smoothly speak indirect but direct.

As I reflect on Mom, she was spiritual, smart, beautiful, talented, classy, balanced, and the best cook ever! Mom was prayerful and studied the Bible daily and committed scriptures to memory. If you only knew the scripture by paraphrase, Mom could tell you exactly where it was found in the Bible. I will always remember she took all of her concerns to God in prayer.

Everyone knew Mom was the best cook ever! One of John's favorites was her cinnamon rolls made from scratch and covered in her homemade icing. She never made a cake without making a sample and we were there to make sure the batter was all out of the bowl. After that, we were the first to get the sample. There was nothing our mom fixed that we did not like—nothing at all she could burn, as John would say. John's favorite meal was chicken and dumplings, and William loved navy beans, onions, and cornbread. Me, I liked it all! She would bake our favorite cake for our birthdays. John's favorite cake was her pound cake. It would melt in your mouth.

Our Mom was a great homemaker who also had excellent taste for fashion. Yes, she was a fashionista of the day. If she bought a new dress, along with that came a new hat from the milliner Ida Lowe, shoes, gloves, purse, the works. She made sure we were dressed appropriately. She passed her sense of style on to us. Not forgetting Dad, he too had a flair for dressing well and checking John and William to make sure they got haircuts weekly and dressed properly.

This I saw in John inasmuch as he was a very fastidious dresser, with a style of his own. He loved shopping in New York and in shops around the world. He knew how to put "the look" together. I remember when the leopard print fashion was "hot." John came home and asked me, "Joyce do you have any of the tiger woman clothes?" I had no idea what he was talking about, so he informed me that women are wearing it. Leopard print (tiger woman clothes as John called it) has kept its popularity and remains a timeless fashion. John had a great eye for fashion. I also remember once John was home for a visit and he told me he needed to go to a shoe shop. He said, "Joyce, you remember Mom taught us never to wear a pair of shoes with run-over heels." He never forgot that, and we got those shoes fixed that day.

Our mom prepared us for the future by imparting essential life skills, teaching us to be self-sufficient in cooking, cleaning, and other aspects that become crucial when living independently away from home. Along with that, Mom and Dad were always focused on instilling within us the value of integrity, guiding us to understand and uphold moral principles and taking responsibility. Early on, we had to earn our allowances, and John and William had jobs cutting yards and they also had paper routes.

Mom served as our church secretary, superintendent of the Sunday school, and our Sunday school teacher. She was a Bible scholar who taught us from a storyteller's point of view that easily captured our attention. I remember her handwriting was impeccable, and she taught us how to write properly. Our parents did a great job preparing us for school. It was not until we were all in school that Mom took a full-time job outside the home.

Dinner time was always special. We ate together in our designated seats around the table, Dad at the head of the table, Mom to his righthand side, me to her right near the kitchen window, and "the boys" on the other side of the table. In the traditional way at that time, all of the food was placed on the table in serving dishes. Dad would bless the food, and each of us would say a short prayer. The three of us always chose the shortest verse in the Bible, "Jesus wept." Once this was done, we would begin the process of passing the dishes around until everyone was served.

There was lots of talk around the table, and this happened not just on Sunday but for breakfast and evening meals each day. There were always several choices during our meals—mashed potatoes, baked potatoes, fresh snapped green beans (we were the snappers), mac and cheese, greens, rice, rice pudding, chicken, steak, cubed steak, porkchops, meatloaf, fish, etc. Mom always said a meal should consist of at least three colors, and ours did just that.

Saturday nights were always special at home. The standard meal was cheese hamburgers and fresh-cut French fries. After that meal, we would make sure we had reviewed our Sunday school lesson and our clothes were ready for church the next day. Then we were ready to join Dad in the living room to watch the boxing matches on the Gillette *Cavalcade of Sports*. Mom would then begin the preparation of the meal for our Sunday dinner, and that was done before bed. When Dad was done, we were allowed to stay awake to watch *Gunsmoke*. While John and I would remain awake, William just could not make it. We would give William a wet towel to moisten his eyes in hopes that he would stay awake. He didn't so we would fill him in on what he missed.

We were fortunate to have incredible parents who loved us unconditionally and guided us in their own unique ways. While Dad took on the role of a disciplinarian, Mom, gentle yet firm, rarely showed frustration. Instead, she consistently demonstrated strength through prayer. As I share this, I think of John during the 9/11 attack. I was told that when the towers were hit, John was asleep. Once he was awakened and understood the magnitude of what was taking place, he fell to his knees and began to pray. That is exactly what Mom would have done.

Our parents transitioned at a young age, Dad on November 16, 1976, at the age of 57 and Mom on June 23, 1982, at the age of 58. The three of us, John, William, and I, would always reminisce about our family life. Losing our parents profoundly altered our lives. In 2005, John and I were the last living members of our biological family. When John became ill, I was frozen with fear. What would I do without him? Sure, caring for John was a challenge, but I would think about the things we learned from Dad and Mom. Yes this was a challenge; however, it was up to me to keep focused and to put one foot in front of the other and do what needed to be done. I am thankful for all the lessons learned. As much as I thought I was not prepared, actually my past had prepared me to step up—afraid or not—to ensure Dad's, Mom's, William's, and finally John's needs were met. This is what families do. This strength came from our parents and by the grace of God. I remain grateful to God for the time we shared and the love and the invaluable gifts and influence our parents bestowed upon us.

Special Occasions

Holidays and birthdays were special times for us growing up. Periodically, relatives would come over to celebrate, but for the most part our celebrations were at our home. We looked forward to all holidays. The ones that stood out most were Valentine's Day, Easter, July Fourth, Halloween, Thanksgiving, and Christmas.

On Valentine's Day we all looked forward to our boxes of candy from Mom and Dad and of course all of the exchange of sugar at school. On one Valentine's Day, my dad surprised our mom with a set of wedding rings. You see, at the time they were married, they had not exchanged rings. I will never forget the look on her face when he gave her that gift.

At Easter we were sure to get new outfits and of course an Easter speech to learn and nervously recite before the whole church. Then there was the Easter egg hunts both at church and at home.

On the Fourth of July, my mom's family had an annual homecoming, and we would go "up home" for the Fourth and spend time with family and friends. There was a lot of food and we were able to shoot fireworks because we were out of the city.

Halloween was an exciting time for us. Mom helped us design our costumes, and we could not wait for nightfall to go trick or treating. We had a designated area where we could go in the neighborhood and then we were off to the Boys Club. The club was always packed with kids on that night. There was so much to see and do. We gained a lot by having the Boys Club in our neighborhood. Imagine a small shotgun house that had once served as the neighborhood school being transformed into a Boys Club. During Halloween, they would have all these different stations around the room where you could play games and have fantastic fun. My favorite things to do were bobbing for apples, fishing coins out of flour, and eating candied apples. Christmas was a blast too, lots of gifts and candy for everyone. This place was fun, and I loved every moment I could be there with my brothers. Though small, it provided lifetime training, experiences, and a protective environment for kids both in and outside the community. Sure, it was fun trick or treating in the neighborhood but much more fun at the Boys Club.

Thanksgiving and Christmas were always big days for us growing up. Mom would prepare those wonderful meals (chicken, ham, turkey and dressing, cranberry sauce, mac and cheese, greens, gravy, homemade yeast rolls, delicious pastries, and more). Mom made the best sweet potato pies with her special recipe, which John kept and made for himself during the holidays. On these and some other holidays, Dad would make homemade ice cream. Mom would mix and boil the custard for the ice cream, and Dad would bring out our hand-cranked ice cream maker. Before we could begin the freezing process, Dad would purchase a block of ice from somewhere, bring it home, chop it up in pieces, and place the ice around the sides of the cylinder. After that, rock salt was poured over the ice. Once all this was in place, Mom would bring the prepared custard, and then the cranking started. We would take turns cranking because we wanted that ice cream ready as soon as possible. It was always delicious.

At Christmas we made our yearly wish list and there was always a live tree decorated and ready for gifts. Mom and Dad would buy our gifts, and we would watch to see when a new gift was added under the tree and then would dash to see whose name was on the tag. We would save our allowance to buy gifts too. I have to admit to this day I can wrap gifts perfectly because a few times my curiosity got away with me wanting to know what was in the packages with my name on them, so I would open and re-wrap it back perfectly. The last time I did that, the boys had bought me a book *Treasure Island*. John busted me out when he caught me re-wrapping their gift. I did not do it again. Most of our gifts were in gift boxes, but Mom always reserved one gift that was rolled and taped on each end. John reminded me how Mom always had a rolled/taped gift for us. John and William were really into football, and I remember the year Mom and Dad bought them an electric football game set. It was amazing to see that board vibrate and the players move down the field. They played for hours.

I will never forget the Christmas Dad placed a large red box under the tree. We had no idea who it was for, so we asked daily. On Christmas day, I found out it was for me! I loved typing, and Dad had bought me an Olivetti-Underwood typewriter. I was so excited—and no, that gift I did not preopen. Today, I still have that typewriter in my office. Again, there were all sorts of gifts during the years—bicycles, clothes, watches, games, toys, the usual; however, one tradition we did not observe was stocking stuffers.

As the years passed and we grew up, I think of things John would do at Christmas. He loved Christmas—and giving gifts was his specialty. He was years ahead of Amazon! I recall during the Christmas holidays, if John did not come home, we always received our gifts on Christmas day. While Amazon was not around then, FedEx would arrive at our door on or before noon Christmas day with our gifts from John. All of the gifts would be wrapped individually and packed into one FedEx box. Believe me, sometimes the box was bulging with only tape holding things inside! It was so much fun to pull out his gifts on Christmas day. He would also remind me that he intentionally wrapped some gifts in Mom's roll and tape style. That memory was priceless. John never forgot Christmas. I still have several of those gifts, and I fondly remember my brother when I use them.

I will always remember the "Figure it out" synthesizer John gave my son, Conrad. In 1994, John spent Christmas at home after returning from Osaka, Japan. While in Japan, John purchased a music synthesizer for which he had lost the instructions while traveling. At that time, Conrad had become interested in music and was writing, arranging, and composing music at age 15. During the visit, Conrad and John had spent time together talking about and playing music. I remember when John was about to walk out the door to catch his plane back to New York, he turned to Conrad with the synthesizer in his hand and said, "Conrad, you take this and figure it out. Conrad figured it out, laying down a lot of beats until it was full.

Lastly, John loved Sims Barbeque. At least three times a year I would send barbeque to New York, either for his personal consumption or for a party. Each time John arrived in Little Rock, our first stop from the airport would be to pick up what he referred to as "Q." He would purchase three or four sandwiches and declare two would be frozen for him to take back to New York. Each time we headed to the airport for his return home, we stopped once again at Sims to pick up his "Q." If you wonder what happened to the frozen sandwiches, don't—he ate them.

Closing my reflections on our family life, I have a collection of specific moments, stories, and experiences while growing up:

Who Is Bubba?

John, affectionately known as Bubba, got his nickname during his early years when our brother, William, could not say "Johnnie." Our mom introduced the nickname Bubba to him. Along with Johnnie and John, Bubba would become one of John's three aliases. While comfortable with his nickname among family and close friends, John preferred to be addressed as John in professional settings and within his musical circles. Our cousin Harry Veronica shared an instance when she called John Bubba while attending a set in the Village. When this happened, she said John politely requested to be called John "in that space." I did the same thing when Dr. Eddie Henderson, a member of the Mingus Band, visited with us in Little Rock at Christmas. During that visit, of course I called John Bubba as I always did. When Eddie heard me use the nickname, and he began using it. I too was corrected. Reflecting on this, my cousin and I came to the conclusion that perhaps John's concern regarding the use of his nickname stemmed from its association with his southern roots (maybe). Anyway, as always John expressed his preference with grace and respect. He was always "My Bubba."

Grocery Shopping

Now this was the best fun ever! On Saturday mornings, our parents would go to the Safeway on Main Street to grocery shop. The rule was that we would remain in the car while Mom and Dad went into the store to shop. We did not mind the wait because we used this time to count cars, identify makes and models of cars, and watch people and whatever else funny came our way. We had no problem entertaining ourselves until our parents returned. During that time, new cars were always released to the public In September. My brothers would quiz me on the different makes and models of cars, and before it was over, I could easily identify the year the car was made and the model. It really did not matter to us that we did not get to go into the store to shop. We just had fun car and people watching. Of course, we had already added our wishes to the grocery list.

The C-L-U-B

I briefly mentioned the Boys Club earlier when talking about our Halloween experiences. I think it is important that you know more about this place we called, "The Club." The Boy's Club was a very special place for my brothers. When headed to the club, they had this ritual of spelling the word "club" out loud as they made their exit: "Where are you going?" "C-L-U-B!" They spent a lot of time there playing sports, learning crafts such as woodworking, creating leather projects, and building relationships with other boys in the community. I always thought it was a great place and I wanted to go there. My brothers were very adamant that this was a place for boys, not girls. We had many arguments about this inconsistency; however, they stood by it and were happy that girls were not allowed. That was the rule back in the day. Fortunately, today that club is for both boys and girls. As I got older, I found out girls were allowed to go to the club two times during the year—Halloween and Christmas. Knowing this, I made it a point to be there for those two occasions.

The Locking Out

After I entered elementary school, my mom took a job and my brothers and I were home during the summer. It was John's responsibility to take care of William and me during our parents' absence. He was to prepare breakfast when we awakened and lunch. This John did each day. However, the argument would ensue when the cleaning would be left to me. I would object some days because I knew they, the boys, were wanting to run out and go to "the club" after lunch and I would be left with the cleanup. I expressed my concern about this, but it fell on deaf ears.

To get their attention when they returned home one day, I locked the doors so they could not come into the house. This was a big problem, and I got in trouble with Dad. After this incident we agreed that we would all work together to clean up the kitchen after the lunch meal and definitely before they went to the Boys Club. For a while, the boys were not talking to me, but they got over It.

Road Trips

As I mentioned before, our parents grew up in Jackson County, and we would make weekend trips at least once or twice a month to Tuckerman where my mom was raised. We would go "up home," as Mom called it. As children, it was okay, but this was the country and a lot of the luxuries that we had at home were not there. It was the first time I saw an outhouse! My dad was raised in Olyphant, but by the time we were born, the town was no more. He would sometimes stop there on the way to Tuckerman and reminisce about growing up. When we would hit a bump or hear a noise as we traveled the highway there, Dad would remind us that he had worked as a laborer building that highway.

Life in the country was so different. Schools were delayed when it was time to pick cotton. I remember one year William decided he was going there to learn to pick cotton to earn money for the summer. John and I told him he was out of his mind; he really did that want to do that. After picking cotton for one day, William was calling home to be picked up. The older we got, we avoided "up home" trips as much as possible.

In 1958, we made my first *real* road trip. We got into our 1957 Plymouth (canary yellow and white) and headed to Chicago to visit my mom's sister, my favorite Aunt Luvenia. I was so excited. I had never been that far away from home before. There was a lot of preparation for this trip, washing, ironing, packing, and of course cooking. I remember Mom made a lunch box for each of us inasmuch as segregation provided few if any places for us to stop to eat. Nevertheless, Mom made sure we had plenty of food for the trip. It was a long ride, but we finally got there. It was a great trip, and we got to see other family members we had not seen and to spend a lot of time with our cousins Herman, James, and Ella Ridley.

Civil Rights

We grew up in the midst of the Civil Rights Movement. Our parents were self-made with great common sense and insight about life. While our dad was very outspoken, Mom was quiet; however, when she spoke, you listened. Both were very intentional and in tune with the times. Our first memory regarding racial injustice was of our dad's fight for civil rights at his job at Dewey Burke Machine Works. He was the only African American working there and his employer, Dewey Burke, would do or say things that he opposed. When this happened, Dad would quit. I can recall several times him coming home and stating, "I quit and I am not going back." Fortunately, he was skilled in what he did and his employer needed him, so Dewey would always make amends and call him back to work.

Our parents were strong in their belief that we honor God and treat others with respect, and they instilled this within us as children growing up. As our mom would always tell us, "If you tell the truth, you do not have to remember what you said."

Another thing I will always remember was during the Central High School crisis in 1957. Dad came home from work earlier than his usual time of 5:15 p.m., and he sat my brothers down—and of course I was there, too. He told them that their activities outside the house would be limited. He wanted to know where they were at all times. I just sat there. I knew something was really wrong. He explained that their safety was very important during these times.

After this serious meeting with "the boys," I then had a side conversation with Dad. I understood why Black students were not welcomed at Central High School and why the U.S. Army's 101st Airborne Division and National Guard (federalized) had been called to Little Rock. Still trying to put everything together,

I looked at my dad, and said, "I do not like Governor Faubus, but I like Governor Eisenhower." Well, you know I got my first Civics lesson that day. That was a family joke for years. My brothers listened to Dad and remained safe during what was a truly dangerous time. Did John and William tease me about this? Yes—for years!

Boss of TV

As I reminisced about our family life, I shared that we were one of the first families to get a television in the neighborhood. With this new television in the house, obviously there was conflict over what shows we would watch. Growing up, William and I looked up to our older brother. John always had an idea about things and how they should run, so he came up with this rule for watching TV. It was called "Boss of TV." Most of the time John and William were in agreement about the shows they wanted to watch, which consisted of cowboy and war movies. I, however, had a desire to watch other things. The game went like this. If you turn on the TV, you are The Boss of the TV; however, if you leave the room for ANY reason, you lose your authority as the Boss and the person who entered the room second would become the Boss. Consequently, if John was the Boss and he left the room, William or I would make it a point to flip the channel to what we wanted. There were times when he tried to change the rule, but I did not go for it. This was a happy game for whomever seized control of the TV. Many times, we had to wait each other out for the cherished title, "Boss of TV." Other times we got in trouble and lost all TV privileges. We tried to prevent this in every way possible.

Boxing Matches

Our dad was a true fan of the *Cavalcade of Sports* sponsored by Gillette. Every weekend, he was spot on looking at the boxing matches. We would join him to watch the fights. Periodically, when our parents were away, my brothers would set up a ring in the kitchen for boxing matches. When this started, I was unaware that I would be the contender with both John and William. As the bouts would begin, things were okay, but then the blows got heavier. It did not take me long to figure out this was not working for me. Why did John and William not box each other? Not getting the right answer to this question, I placed them both on notice that I would no longer participate in the boxing matches.

We used to look back on those days and laugh. They said they were sure I would go along with it, but I did not. I can recall, if I got hit hard on the chin, John would rush to get water to slap on the area and tell me everything was okay. As I think back, I must have been out of my mind going along with this idea. I guess in those days they were preparing me for the future. I now train with coach Anthony Tucker at Straightright Boxing & Fitness in Little Rock where I am learning the true science of boxing.

The Birthday Story

Growing up, John was always very easy going. He and William were approximately two years apart in age. As far as I can remember, they were close and did everything together. I sometimes felt left out because "those boys" (as my mom referred to them) got to do things I could not do. Baby sisters can be a challenge, and I know I was when I came into the family in 1951. Through the years on my birthday, John would retell the story of my birth in specific detail. It went like this…

Mom and Dad went to the hospital when it was time for my birth. Upon returning from United Friends Hospital, which was located on Ninth Street, there I was—this little baby girl dressed in pink. John stated he and William kept looking at me and asked Mom and Dad if I was going to stay. They said, "Yes, this is your new baby sister." He said they had concerns about having a girl around. After all, prior to my birth, it was just the two of them and this was all new to them.

John said I was so little and all he could remember was this pink satin outfit I was wearing with a pink satin bonnet on my head. They just did not know what to think. There were times growing up when my brothers would try to make me believe I was adopted, but they knew I was not buying it.

I looked forward to this story every year from John. I miss hearing him tell it, but I am thankful for all the times he did share it. During John's last visit home in March of 2003, he shared the story once again, and we took a picture holding the pink outfit I came home in. That was the last time he told the story.

I felt deeply loved by my brothers. John's annual sharing about my birth and our early years together was heartwarming. Growing up, it seemed like I had three fathers. As the oldest, John gracefully embraced the challenge of setting an example for us with both humility and love.

Life in the Village

As I reminisce about our childhood, I acknowledge that life wasn't perfect; however, the memories are priceless. Our upbringing was shaped by the love and guidance of our parents, who imparted invaluable lessons along the way. The neighborhood and schools formed a tight knit community where children could roam freely, enveloped by a sense of freedom and security. Neighbors played a significant role; offering guidance when necessary and acting as an extended family.

At home, our needs were effortlessly met, thanks to Dad and Mom's ability to manage finances. I do not recall hearing them discuss finances instead they provided what we needed and often what we wanted, leaving us with a sense of knowing all was well.

II. Spiritual Journey

Our parents did not attend the same church. Our dad was a member of St. Mark Baptist Church, which we could see out of our front door. We attended the Holiness Church on Fulton Street one block east of our home with our mom. Only on occasions did we attend church with Dad and he with us. We attended Sunday school and church on a regular basis. Early on, we all memorized the Lord's Prayer and the 23rd Psalm. These were our bedtime prayers each night.

The Holiness Church was known for long services on Sunday. The church believed in making a joyful noise unto the Lord, and that they did. There was a lot of praying, singing, testifying, shouting, prophesying, and outreach into the community to tell others about the goodness of God and how to be saved.

We would attend Sunday school where our mom served as our Sunday school teacher. The Sunday service began with not less than 20 minutes of prayer on our knees, then there was singing and music where people would give their personal testimony. Before testifying, many would sing their own song of choice which could go on for a long time. After that, the offering would be taken (more songs), and finally the minister would preach until at least 3:00 p.m. We were always glad to get home to eat, and dinner was always ready because Mom cooked on Saturday. We would return to church at 6:30 p.m. to Young People Willing Workers (YPWW) and a sermon that usually put us back home around 9:00.

During the week there was a regular service on Wednesday night, Home and Foreign Mission on Thursday night, and regular service again on Friday night. As children, we had another service on Saturday during the day that was called Junior Church. There we were taught about the Bible, learned the books in the Bible, and had Bible drills to test our knowledge on where to find scriptures and how fast we could do it. During the summer, the church would reach out to children in the community, and we would have Vacation Bible School. "Yes, we spent a lot of time in church growing up."

Without a doubt all of this time spent in church was a great influence on John's life. There was always a lot of music and singing. As time went on, a junior choir was started at the church, and we had choir practice on Saturday. We all sang in the choir including John. One song that John and I talked about as adults was called "Packing Up." We would sing that song and set the church on fire. We never forgot the words, and we would sing it together as we reminisced.

I recall John telling me about a lady at our church who played saxophone. He said this lady was mean, and we would stay out of her way. John talked about how she would pull the horn out of the case, put the mouthpiece on, and connect the neck strap to the instrument. In his mind, she looked and acted so mean toward kids, he felt sure she had bent the bell of the horn. Whatever the case, John said this woman could really play that horn. He was really drawn to her playing—this was his introduction to the saxophone and he never forgot it. John told me that he felt sorry that the woman would bend the bell of the horn.

Our mom's friend Clara Howard was the pianist at the church. She was blind, but how she could play the piano. She would visit our home frequently, and we loved to hear her play and sing—"Touch Me, Lord Jesus." It amazed us how she could not see, but she played beautifully. John often reminded me that when Mom was not in the room, she would sing and play the blues for him. Music took firm root for John during this time and it stayed in his head—all of the music experienced in the church, music lessons, and the TV were great influencers in what was to come in John's life.

As John got older, playing non-church music became a challenge. He had discussed with our parents his desire to play secular music, and our mom's response was that the music he was engaging in was the "devil's music" and that he should focus on playing "church music" rather than in clubs.

Our dad initially felt that John should continue to play his music, but he should seek other employment in order to make a living. I could see that Dad felt that getting a steady Monday-through-Friday job was what John needed to do in the future. This was just the thing a young man was supposed to do. Get a job and earn money. Playing music was not going to meet that end. John continued to demonstrate to them how he felt about the music and that this was what he wanted to do. As time went on, our parents relented little by little, and John proceeded to perfect the music he enjoyed, engaging with other musicians and bands, and eventually, in his teens, he was on the Ninth Street circuit playing with local bands and hearing the music of many of the master musicians who traveled through Little Rock on the Chitlin Circuit (e.g., Duke Ellington, Wilson Pickett, Don Byas, etc.). While it was initially a challenge to convince our parents of his true desire for music, with time and persistence he was able to show them where his passion was, and they eventually came to understand even if they did not agree.

John would come home and tell us about his experiences and the different musicians with whom he had played. Dad was a Big Band fan, and when he heard about his favorites, I could tell he was proud of John. While Mom thought that church music was best, she too respected how John felt. By the time the pressures of these challenges lifted, John was already immersed in his passion and his intensive focus on playing "the music." This all began in the church where there was a lot of singing, the Junior Choir, and several instruments, e.g., tambourines, guitars, drums, piano, organ. Lest we forget the mean lady on the saxophone. Without a doubt, the church was a major influence in shaping John's musical identity. From time to time John would say to me, "Joyce, the music I play is unto the Lord."

III. Education

Again, Mom and Dad were our first teachers. They knew life was complicated, so they used every opportunity to lead by example, teaching us about honoring God, being truthful, helping others, and taking our education seriously. This was just a way of life for us and we took it seriously. While our parents' education ended at the eighth grade, they knew far more. They knew life from a holistic and simplistic view point, and they generously shared that with us. After our parents transitioned, John and I would always talk about how great they were and how thankful we were that they provided us with so much to take our place in this world—truly knowledge far beyond an education. Mom called it "Mother Wit." Now let me open door to take a look at John's educational journey—elementary, junior high school, high school, college, and his early music experiences.

John entered Booker T. Washington Elementary School in 1951. His first teacher was Miss Hill, and his best friend was Fred Carter. This, Mom recorded once again in his baby book. John completed grades first through sixth at Booker T. Washington School, where music was a big part of his education. He often recalled some of the songs sung in elementary school. This along with his musical experience from church stayed in his head. Music was always in his life. He told me our dad told him that our grandfather Johnnie Stubblefield wanted a band, and he envisioned his nine children being members of the band.

When John was nine, Mom placed him in private piano lessons with Edna Douglas, a local musician who lived a few blocks from our house. Later William and I were added to the music lessons team. Mrs. Douglas was both an accomplished pianist and vocalist, and had received her training from the Chicago Conservatory. She was a perfectionist who drove home the need for her students to learn to read, play, write music, respect tempo, and by all means arrive on time for lessons ($1.00 per lesson).

I later learned that it was John's fourth-grade teacher who encouraged Mom to get him involved in music to encourage him to focus better on his school work. Just as those lessons began, our parents purchased an upright Kimball piano. It was huge! We were so excited to have our own piano in our house.

John and I would often talk about how Mrs. Douglas's music room was set up. She emptied her living room and placed her black baby grand piano in the corner of the room and took her dining room and kitchen chairs and set them in a semicircle in the room. As students came in, they would take their seat in the next open chair, and that determined the order in which they received lessons. This was a little intimidating because if the room was full and it was time for your lesson, all eyes were on you—heaven forbid if you had not practiced.

I will never forget Mrs. Douglas would put an egg in a glass of milk and drink it while conducting lessons. Eww, that was something to see, but she did it. At first, we all practiced regularly; however, as time went on, William and I lost interest. After finishing book two of John Schaum and the addition of the Broadman Hymnal, I decided this music thing was not what I wanted. But not John—he loved it! Mrs. Douglas saw John's ability early on. She inspired and encouraged him to understand the music. Mrs. Douglas continued to have an impact on the lives of many students throughout Little Rock, several of whom went on to become musicians for their churches and other venues. Thankfully, it is with Mrs. Douglas that John began to develop his ability to read and understand music and he later used those skills learned from her to write and compose music. This introduction to piano served as a true harbinger of what was to come in John's life as a professional musician.

Band

Upon graduation from elementary school, John entered Dunbar Junior High School in 1957 when he was 12 years old. This is where his fascination with music really took off. John joined the band right away, and I remember when he brought his first instrument home—a flute-a-phone. It was ivory in color with deep burgundy trim. When I picked it up, it felt heavy in my hands. It was definitely well made. John would run the scales with little effort. It was so easy for him. He would let me try to play it, but of course, I made all sorts of wild sounds—nothing like John's.

When John entered junior high, he made his switch from piano to tenor saxophone. Mrs. Douglas was not happy with his decision. When John passed her house on the way home from school, he told me she would remind him from time to time that he should return to his piano lessons. Not John, he had found what he wanted, the saxophone.

John went on to study saxophone at Dunbar Junior High School and Horace Mann High School in Little Rock, and was active in both the concert bands and marching bands.

The band was just where John wanted to be. He often told me the story of his journey to the tenor saxophone. He said he rushed into the band room and picked the baritone saxophone, thinking it was the same instrument as that of the "mean saxophone player from church." Soon he found he had made a mistake; he had *not selected* the tenor saxophone. His classmate Tyrone Shaw had selected the tenor saxophone! Realizing his mistake, he went to Tyrone and they agreed to exchange instruments. It was on from there.

His first band directors were Leon Adams and Sylvia Clay. John said his band directors were young and progressive, and he learned to both play and read music fast which allowed them to play early on with upper class band members. These band directors were very young, perhaps just seven or eight years older than their students. This was a plus for the students because this was a time when the world was shifting in many ways and these teachers were progressive and were open to thinking more on the student's level and allowed the students to be creative.

Leon Adams wanted to introduce John the clarinet, but John had no intentions of any other instrument taking the place of his tenor sax at that time. Later, John did perfect the clarinet, flute, alto and soprano sax, flugelhorn, French horn, and of course the piano.

As John got into the music, the borrowed instrument from the band room was not enough. John went to our parents and asked if they would buy a saxophone for him. My parents made it happen, and I remember the day we went to Rosen Music Company to look at this Selmer tenor saxophone. I wandered around the store while the purchase was made. Monthly payments were set up, and John had his first saxophone. Talk about happy—he was elated. His instrument and neck strap were always close by.

John met and became lifelong friends with John Bush III (who we will call JB) at Dunbar Junior High. It was during this friendship John discovered that JB's aunt was married to the saxophonist Don Byas. *Imagine that!* At the early age of 12, John meets a relative of Don Byas, the jazz tenor saxophonist who played with the masters—Count Basie, Duke Ellington, Art Blakely, Dizzy Gillespie, and others. When John and JB hooked up, they were listening to music and gaining more and more knowledge about the world of jazz.

As time progressed John's talent continued to grow. Wherever he went, if he did not have his instrument with him, the neck strap was with him. I know our neighbors wanted us to move because he practiced day in and day out. While at Dunbar, John, JB, and a few others got together and created their own band.

This band would play for weekend socials, assemblies, and other affairs at school. Both John and JB recalled their favorite tune was "Honky Tonk" by Bill Doggett. JB shared that during one of the assemblies they had a challenge because a girl (I. J. Routen) wanted to play with the band, but they were not for it. I. J. won out when Mrs. Clay, the band director, allowed her to join the band and play in the assembly with the guys. Now they had two females in the band—Mrs. Clay accompanied them on piano. For years JB said he and John would tease each other about this incident. "After all," JB stated, "The guys thought they were the cat's meow."

My brother's love for "the music" was unquenchable. He listened to the music over and over again. He studied the masters. He played the music. JB said that while he was learning the basic cords associated with jazz music, John was playing the cords of the accomplished musicians. JB said he told John that they needed to learn the basics. John responded he was starting at the top and would backfill to the basics later.

It was during these years that our house became a gathering place for young musicians in and outside the neighborhood. There was a lot of land around our house where we had plenty of space to roam. We rode our bikes, played on our gym set, and played sports and hide and seek, but John used this space for listening, practicing, playing, discussing music, and having jam sessions for hours. It was a plus that our house was the last house on the block. These jam sessions were a weekly occurrence; I suppose the neighbors became accustomed to this and did not complain about the music.

It was magical for John. He heard the music in his head constantly, and when he picked up his instrument, he played it. It was always fascinating that Little Rock was on the Chitlin Circuit. As a result, many master musicians came through and played on Ninth

Street. John was there watching and listening around the age of 15. He absorbed all of the music he could latch on to. This was great for John, and by the time he entered high school, he was already perfecting his art. After all, he was listening to jazz artists as early as age 11 or 12.

John entered Horace Mann High School after graduating from Dunbar, and his intense study of "The Music" continued to grow while playing in the Concert and Marching bands. When he graduated from high school, he received a music scholarship to AM&N College, now known as the University of Arkansas at Pine Bluff (UAPB). John graduated from AM&N in 1967.

IV. Musical Voyage Begins

John bought his first album at the age of 14. At that time he was listening to a variety of artists like Nat King Cole, Tommy Dorsey, and what were called variety shows on TV, etc. During his senior year and throughout college, he toured the South and Midwest with various rhythm and blues bands, including such top artists as The Drifters, Little Junior Parker, Solomon Burke, O. V. Wright, and Jackie Wilson. In 1963, he also worked as a studio musician at Stax Records in Memphis and recorded with York Wilburn and the Thrillers. He was establishing his pattern of playing with many musicians in a variety of styles, from R&B and gospel to modern jazz. While in college, one of his band directors worked as a promoter associated with bands traveling on the Chitlin' Circuit. He would hire John and other musicians at the school to travel to various locations in Tennessee, Mississippi, and Arkansas where John met and played with many musicians.

What is the Chitlin' Circuit? During segregation Black entertainers could not perform in white clubs; consequently, they developed certain areas in the South, East, and Midwest to which they traveled to perform. The routes they toured were called the Chitlin' Circuit. Some of the clubs on Ninth Street where famous musicians such as Duke Ellington, Billie Holiday, Count Basie, Al Hibbler, Richard Boone, and others played were the Flamingo, El Dorado, Safari, and Kings Court. John began playing at the Flamingo around age 15 with York Wilburn and the Thrillers.

Before winning our parents over to play on Ninth Street, John would sneak there and listen to the music. Later at the early age of 15 or 16, he became a part of the mix.

I remember one of John's gigs at the Flamingo where he had a cool outfit—a gold glitter-like tuxedo jacket with black slacks, satin lapels, white shirt, cuff links, black bowtie—"the works." I had never seen anything like this before other than on TV. The bling was exciting, so exciting. I saw John after he got dressed that night for the gig. He looked great in this "gig outfit" and wingtip shoes shined to the point they looked like glass. Off he went to his gig.

I recall early on when John started performing publicly, he was getting ready to leave for a gig. While preparing, he was talking with Mom while his horn case lay open. She noticed a bottle of Pepto Bismol inside. When she asked about it, John explained that he would drink it to calm his queasy stomach before performances. As time went on, this remedy was short-lived, as John continued to engage and captivate audiences with his stellar performances, no more butterflies.

Again, John attended AM&N College on a music scholarship where he studied other woodwind instruments and played in the orchestra and marching band. In 1967 John won the "Outstanding Soloist Award" at the Little Rock Intercollegiate Jazz Festival. He formed the quintet The New Directions, which in 1969 was commissioned by the University of Arkansas to tour England, Russia, and the Middle East. In 1989, the New Directions Quintet was again honored by the University with a 20th Year reunion concert.

After graduation from AM&N College with a bachelor of arts in music, John moved immediately to Chicago where he joined the Association for the Advancement of Creative Musicians (AACM), which at that time was at the peak of its activity. In addition to studying the Schillinger system of composition for a year with Muhal Richard Abrams, he played in and composed for the AACM Big Band, recorded for Delmark with fellow members

Maurice McIntyre and Joseph Jarman, and Henry Threadgill, and led his own ensembles. During this period, John also did course work toward a master of arts at Vandercook College in Chicago and the University of Indiana. He also taught in the Chicago Public School system under a federally-funded music program.

Chicago was a good stopping point in John's life. He served as an itinerate music teacher there, and this allowed him to move to different schools throughout the city. This is where he met and married his only wife, Sharon Seabury. I would spend time in Chicago visiting John and my Aunt Luvenia and cousin Ella during many spring and summer breaks while in college. This is when I first met Sharon. She is a brilliant and fascinating woman and an extraordinary educator. During one visit to Chicago, I got to meet Sharon for the first time. John talked about her often, and I already had the feeling they would marry soon. When we met, I asked Sharon if she knew John's first love, she softly looked at me and said, "I know." John and Sharon were married in 1971, and from that union, my nephew John C. Stubblefield was born. For years, I believed the "C" in John's middle name stood for Cornelius, our dad's middle name. However, in a conversation with Sharon, she told me that the "C" was not for our dad's name. Instead, it was for Coltrane, a tribute to John's admiration for the jazz legend. Sharon emphasized that this was what John wanted when his son was born.

I remember when John was living in Chicago, someone broke into his apartment and stole his instrument. He called home and was very upset that this had happened. While this might have served as a challenge, he replaced the instrument quickly. The challenge was not the "break in." It was breaking in the new instrument to make it what he wanted it to be—and that he did.

During my interviews, Ben Jones, one of the members of the New Directions Quintet, revealed the full story about the break in. While he was visiting with John, he accidently left the apartment and thought the door was locked when in fact it was not. Ben shared that he felt bad about the theft, but he said not once did John put him down or hold this over his head. This was how John rolled. This was his vibe—all was well.

The music was always meant for John. He heard it in his head constantly, and when he picked up his instrument, he played it. I recall he phoned me one day and we were on one of our many marathon conversations. Along the way, he stopped and asked me to hold on. He was gone much longer than I expected. I continued to hold on but thought about hanging up several times. When he finally returned, I asked, "Where have you been?"

He replied, "There was a bird outside the window humming a melody, and I wanted to write it down." I then told him, "The next time you want to do that, don't leave me on hold. Just call me back." I remember ending the call and thinking about how serious he was about "the music"—so serious that he couldn't fail to capture the melody of a bird perched outside his window. Wow!

Finally, I remember the day John Coltrane died. He was paramount in John's life. John listened, played, studied, and wrote his music over and over again. I was 16 years old when I received a call from John on July 17, 1967. He told me while he was riding home on a city bus he heard of Coltrane's death and all he could do was cry. I could tell he was very sad, and I just listened to him talk it out. We used to call this "getting it all out." This was truly a sad day for John.

Chicago was a stepping stone for bigger and better things for John. While there he experienced all forms of the arts and built a foundation for that broad musical base he would stand on for the rest of his life. He grew in his art and continued to pursue his dream, going to New York "where the music is." In 1971 he and John and Sharon took the plunge. They sold everything and moved to New York—after all, "that was where the music is." As life goes, Chicago had its high and low points. It was time to leave

Chicago and John was ready. It was here, as our dad would say, John got his feet wet, and in New York not only did he get his feet wet, he was totally immersed in the water.

John was always thoughtful of others and was consistent in letting them know. Here are more personal recollections about things that occurred during his years in Chicago.

My High School Graduation

John had established himself in Chicago, "the windy city," and bought his first car in 1969. It was a 1969 charcoal and gray Javelin (muscle car) with a red pinstripe. He surprised me by driving home for my graduation from Central High School in May 1969. I was so excited that he came home to see me graduate! The ceremony was held at the Barton Coliseum, which was a large venue where we had our yearly State Fair. I can hear his voice now! There were approximately 800 people in my class. Since my last name started with an S, it was well into the night before I was called. I recall when I stepped across the stage to get my diploma, I heard this loud voice calling my name. I knew it was my brother sounding the alarm for me as I accomplished that milestone. I could always count on him; he was always there to cheer me on.

"You've Got Mail!"

While I was in college, I noticed that John would always write to me or send me some information about music or an item he had picked up for me during his many tours. Once while I was thanking him for the mail, he said to me, "Joyce, I have always known that you like mail, and I make sure you are receiving it while you are in college." I was amazed. I had no idea he knew that about me. I did enjoy receiving mail, and my brother made sure I did just that.

For the rest of his life, John continued to keep the mail flowing to me. As he traveled the world, he sent postcards! I have postcards and letters from all over the world. As I think about it, it was not just postcards. It was letters, cards for all holidays—birthdays, Valentine's Day, St. Patrick's Day, Easter, Mother's Day, Anniversaries, Christmas, and just thinking-of-you cards. I kept those cards and continue to pull them out and read them during holidays.

Once while traveling, he forgot to get a card for my birthday, so he merely designed his own card on paper and sent it to me. He loved to celebrate and stay in contact with people with letters, cards, and postcards. He never forgot to celebrate his family, friends, and musicians in some way throughout the year. He was a giver, and he gave himself to others in so many ways—most importantly through "the music."

I recall talking with Sue Mingus when John was ill. She told me, "Joyce, we miss John so much. He was the life of the band. He never forgot a birthday of a member. Even while on the road he managed to find a cake to celebrate."

I remember when John was traveling in Europe on his 50th birthday and how much I worked to make sure he too would be celebrated for this milestone birthday. Somehow, we pulled it off and he was surprised! Sue assured me he was greatly celebrated on his 50th.

A Way with Words

John and I would spend hours on the phone talking. It was during these conversations he would fill me in on the music, his arranging, composing, travels and expected engagements, plays on Broadway, restaurants, cooking, etc.—you name it, we talked for hours. And if he was reading a book, he would briefly tell me about it and in a few days, I would get a copy in the mail. It was interesting to find that he had one other friend and fellow musician who shared his love for books and music, and they too spent many hours on the phone—Oliver Gatto. As I reviewed John's recordings in his day books from 1974–2004, there were entries showing he and Oliver had talked long hours constantly between New York and Paris.

Regarding words, John was notorious for making up words during our conversations. One day while talking, I suppose I mentioned I felt like I was coming down with a cold. Immediately he said to me, "Joyce, you have to get some Oscillococcinum." I said to him, "There you go again making up words." He replied, "No, no, I am for real. This stuff is really good. I take it all the time if I am feeling sick." I just could not believe that was a word. But, as I always did when John told me something, I went to the drug store, and believe it or not, there it was—OSCILLOCOCCINUM. What a word. I continue to take the big "O" from that day until now. I shared it with friends, many of whom probably thought I too was making up a word. While visiting in Chicago, I told my friend Bea Klokpah about Oscillococcium. At that time, she was preparing to travel internationally for a month. Upon returning, she said to me, "Joyce, I took Oscillococcium while on my trip, and I did not get sick one time, even with Covid all around." I was surprised she had remembered to take this wonder medicine on her trip. While it was funny to hear John make up words, I am glad this word was real.

V. New York and the World

John always said the music was in New York and that was where he was going. Shortly after their marriage, John and Sharon set off on the long drive from Chicago to New York City. Sharon said prior to the move, John had meticulously mapped out the trip, secured a beautiful apartment on the East Side, and was prepared for this long-anticipated new phase of life. He had been in contact with various musicians who had encouraged the move and promised leads.

Upon arriving, Sharon described things as being very different. I laughed when she said John was driving through red lights trying to keep up with the rhythm of the busy New York traffic patterns. She further said that when they arrived, there were challenges far greater than expected, but John did not let that stop him. She said he was a planner, and he used his contact list and continued to network, and doors began to open. Upon their arrival in New York, there was a telephone strike and there was no way to reach anyone by phone. Mary Lou Williams found out John was in town and sent him a telegram inviting him to his first gig. After moving to New York John continued his work in the modern and avant-garde jazz scenes. He became affiliated with Jazz Interactions, Jazz Composer's Orchestra Association, Collective Black Artists, and the Jazz Repertory Company. He began working with the Charles Mingus band in 1972 when he was 28 years old. After five months in the band, there was a disagreement between John and Mingus which lead to John being blacklisted in the New York jazz community. He never shared with me what occurred between them that led to the break. Interviews indicate although John left the band, Mingus did reach out and ask John to return, but he declined. Again, I do not know the reason, but knowing John, something was not right with the music and John stood firm.

John did not allow this situation to stop him from moving forward. Instead, he used this opportunity to make other contacts and play with other bands. From 1971 to 1975, he performed and toured nationally with Mary Lou Williams, Henry Threadgill, Charles Mingus, the Thad Jones and Mel Louis Orchestra, the Gil Evans Orchestra, Frank Foster's Big Band, Fort Apache Band, and Bill Hardman. He also recorded with Miles Davis, McCoy Tyner, Dollar Brand (Abdullah Ibrahim), Anthony Braxton, Roy Brooks, M'tume, Reggie Lucas, and Lester Bowie.

In 1974, he toured Europe with the Gil Evans Orchestra, Dollar Brand's African Space Program. That same year he also joined the faculty of the New York City Jazzmobile, where he taught for more than 20 years, lecturing, leading seminars, and conducting workshops throughout the world. During 1974 and 1975, he was a member of Cecil McBee's Sextet and of Dr. Billy Taylor's band before joining Nat Adderley and the Basic Black Band with whom he recorded and toured the U.S. from 1975 to 1977.

Throughout his career, John had numerous international tours in Europe, Africa, Japan, Russia, India, Asia, Australia, New Zealand, and beyond. He also performed in major jazz festivals, including many appearances—Montreux , Black Sea, Verona, New Orleans, Newport, Red Sea, etc. Throughout this period, he continued to develop his versatility, performing in a number of Broadway shows and working with such popular artists as Marvin Gaye and Diana Ross. On three separate occasions (1973, 1976, and 1978), he won the *Down Beat* Critics' Poll for "Talent Deserving Wider Recognition."

He recorded at New York's Town Hall with another former member of AACM, free jazz innovator Anthony Braxton. He also played with legendary Latin jazz performer and band leader Tito Puente, as well as Kenny Baron, McCoy Tyner, Freddie Hubbard, and the World Saxophone Quartet.

VI. Jazz Globetrotter

After four years in New York, the music had taken off and John was busy doing what he loved, writing, composing, recording, and playing "The Music." In 1975, John produced his first album as a leader, *Midnight Sun* (released in 1980 on Sutra Records), and in 1976 recorded *Prelude* for Storyville Records. Like his subsequent recordings, these albums featured his own compositions. His works have also been performed and recorded by many other artists, from Mary Lou Williams and Hank Crawford to Roy Haynes, Kenny Barron, Billy Hart, and Jerry Gonzalez.

John formed his own quartet in 1980, which over the years included such members as Albert Dailey, Cecil McBee, Victor Lewis, Mulgrew Miller, Marvin "Smitty" Smith, Mike Nock, George Cables, Keith Copeland, and Clint Houston. Also, John toured the U.S. with George Russell, Louis Hayes, Kenny Barron, and the World Saxophone Quartet.

From 1979 to 1983, he was saxophonist and musical director of Reggie Workman's group, Top Shelf. In 1982, he and Harry Whitaker also co-led the band Giant Steps, which included Anthony Jackson, John Lee, J. T. Lewis, and Victor Lewis. That same year, he composed a jingle for a Revlon product, Esteem men's cologne. In 1983 John served for a time as Jazz Ensemble Director for Rutgers University. That year, the Rutgers Jazz Ensemble won the Notre Dame Intercollegiate Jazz Festival, a first for the Rutgers Music Department.

In the fall of 1984, John again toured Europe and was a regular performer on the Continent as a leader and with other well-known artists including Randy Weston, Freddy Hubbard, the World Saxophone Quartet, Kenny Barron, Henry Threadgill, Jerry Gonzales and the Fort Apache Band, Charlie Haden, and McCoy Tyner. In 1986, John made his first tour of Japan with Teruo Nakamura's Rising Sun Band. In 1988, he returned twice to Asia: once with Kenny Barron to India and once with Manterio, Young, and Holt to Singapore. One of his favorite international spots was in Osaka, Japan.

In 1984, John recorded *Confessin'* for Soul Note Records, then in 1986, his first album for Enja, *Bushman Song*, followed by *Countin' on the Blues* the next year. John recorded more than 20 albums during the 1980s, working with such artists as Teo Macero, Kenny Barron, Julius Hemphill, Oliver Lake, Jerry Gonzales, Louis Hayes, Abdullah Ibrahim, and Teruo Nakamura.

For John, the 1990s held the promise of continued success as a leader, performer, composer, and arranger. His eighth album, *Sophisticated Funk*, was released in 1990 on Cheetah Records. In concerts, clubs, and at festivals, the John Stubblefield Quartet remained active in the U.S. and Europe. His sextet, Quiet Fire, featured Virgil Jones and Eddie Henderson on trumpet, Gayton Thurman and Jason Jackson on trombone, Cecil McBee on bass, Johnathan Blake and Victor Lewis on drums, and George Caligan and Hubert Eaves on piano. A highlight in 1992 for his sextet was the performance of the music of Miles Davis's *Kind of Blue* at Medgar Evers College. John not only recorded with Miles; he also spoke about attending frequent jam sessions with Miles in their neighborhood. John told me that Miles advised him that he needed more patience and he could develop that patience by learning to cook, a lesson John took to heart.

In 2001, Mitchell Seldel quoted John this way in an article regarding the inception of Quiet Fire:

"After traveling with McCoy Tyner, Kenny Barron, the Mingus Big Band, the Fort Apache Band, I decided to put a new book together of my compositions—new and old pieces that I've played and recorded, and to open a forum for other musicians to write for this band." The 18-month-old band's repertoire included tunes from the entire history of jazz, plus "we do covers of rhythm and blues and pop songs. We'll spring one of those out every now and then," he added. Stubblefield said shifting to a leader status from other varied work, "is not that different. I had a lot of time with McCoy's band working as a straw boss in his big band and here now, it's new in the fact that I'm doing it with six pieces as opposed to 14."

Also in 1992, John returned to Japan with the all-star "Chasin' The Trane" Tour, performing the music of John Coltrane. John remained a regular member of the McCoy Tyner Big Band, Grammy Award winners in 1993 for their album *Turning Point*. John was a member, as well, of the Kenny Barron Quintet, the Billy Hart Sextet, and Jerry Gonzalez and Fort Apache, and continued to perform with the World Saxophone Quartet. As a teacher, John had served over 20 years at Jazzmobile, lecturing, leading 58 seminars, and conducting workshops throughout the world. In 1993 John recorded again for Enja with a quartet featuring George Cable, Victor Lewis, and Clint Houston. The resulting CD, *Morning Song*, released in 1994 has been highly praised by critics. In 1995, the John Stubblefield Quartet made its debut in Australia.

While there was a split between Charles Mingus and John in the early years, John returned to the Mingus Band in the 90s and was instrumental in preserving the legacy of the renowned bassist and composer. After Mingus's death, his widow, Sue Mingus, founded a big band in Mingus's honor. John led the Mingus Big Band for over 13 years and was the only member who had actually played with Mingus. John was a dedicated bandleader and steward of the Mingus legacy. When John transitioned, Sue said to me, "The band will never be the same without John."

From the late 70's until 2004, John embarked on numerous international trips, enduring grueling journeys involving various modes of transportation such as buses, trains, planes, and boats. Whenever he had tours abroad, we would discuss his itinerary so I could keep track of his whereabouts and know how to reach him. I vividly recall one day receiving an international call while at work. Upon answering, the caller immediately asked, "Are you the next of kin of John Stubblefield?" Those words filled me with apprehension, and I quickly asked about John's well-being. As it turned out, during that tour in Russia, all of John's identification had been stolen. The call I received was to confirm his identity for the issuance of new documents. John later explained while walking on the street his leather crossbody bag had been cut away and stolen. To prevent such incidents in the future, I found a travel sport coat that could securely hold all of his personal papers—that was a frightening ordeal.

Even while jazz globetrotting, John always took steps to protect his embouchure. During his illness, I noted he would floss his teeth consistently each day. I can see him now, holding up a CD as if it were a mirror and flossing away. I thought it was his way of dealing with stress. I shared my observation with one of the musicians, and he told me that John flossed his teeth consistently in order to keep his teeth strong. He reminded me there was no way John could play his instruments as he did if his teeth and gums were not strong.

Not only did John meticulously care for his teeth, but he also held a deep reverence for the preparation of reeds for his various instruments. During one of our many conversations, he talked about the shift in the availability from cane to synthetic reeds due to the shortage of cane. John felt strongly that cane reeds produced a superior sound quality. In an article published by Woodwinds & Brass regarding Cane vs. Synthetic it stated the following, "There are advantages and disadvantages to both. On a great cane reed, the sound is warmer, the response is even through all registers, the sax player has a good sense of control over the sound, and the experience is amazing. All this said, regarding a 'great' cane reed." This I believe affirms John's preference for the cane reed.

John's dedication to perfecting the use of cane reeds was evident in his extensive collection of reeds, including unopened reeds for his saxophone, alto saxophone, and clarinet, bought during his European travels. Interviews will reveal John's routine of shaving and sanding reeds to achieve perfection and ensuring he always had an ample supply for performances. After all, the sound was everything....

There are two more things about John and his musical journey. Number one, during one of John's visits home, he dedicated himself to mastering the technique of circular breathing. Each day, I listened as he practiced, but initially, he told me he struggled to grasp the concept. Upon returning to New York, he called to let me know he had achieved his goal. He now understood the mechanics of gathering and holding his breath which enabled him to hold notes indefinitely. This skill became evident in his performances, where he effortlessly held notes for extended durations, as seen in various video recording. When John came home as a featured guest musician at the Wildwood Festival in Little Rock, he conducted a master class where he generously shared his knowledge of circular breathing with young musicians in attendance. During this master class, his junior high school band teacher, Leon Adams, was there and saw John's expertise firsthand. The second intriguing aspect of John's persona was his love for hats of all styles and shapes. Throughout his career, he amassed a diverse collection of hats, each adding flair to his distinctive appearance.

John settled in New York in 1971. He had arrived in the city *"where the music is."* He found the city to exceed his expectations, ultimately making it his permanent residence. Below are some personal reflections I recall during his time in New York.

The Business Trip

During a business trip to New York in the mid-90s, John decided to spend the morning showing me and my colleague around the city. We started on a whirlwind journey using every mode of transportation available—walking, subway, bus, taxi, and at the end he sent us to the airport in a limousine. John took us on a tour that covered upper, mid, and lower Manhattan, including iconic landmarks such as the Empire State Building, World Trade Center, Harlem, Ellis Island, Broadway, Katz Delicatessen and the various clubs where he performed. Despite the packed itinerary, we had to keep moving as we had a plane to catch that evening. I remember John proposing that we enter the World Trade Center; however, rather than going inside, we observed crowds of people moving about from the outside. By the end of the tour, we were exhausted and grateful to board our plane just to get some rest. However; John's energy remained high as he saw us off to LaGuardia Airport. It was an exhilarating day, thanks to my big brother ensuring we experienced the City.

Positive Thinking

John was an avid reader of numerous books. He and I spent hours on the phone talking about books we were reading, as well as about traveling, current and past events, etc. We talked about everything. In today's terms, we served as each other's therapist. If I had something bugging me I knew I could talk it over with him. *The Power of Positive Thinking* is one book we passed back and forth between the two of us. If I was moaning about something, he would direct me back to reading that book, and on the other hand we would send each other copies of the book if it had been misplaced. I still have my last copy from John.

Where Are the Books

As my career progressed, I started to think about building a consulting business of my own. John and I would discuss my goals and how I would accomplish them. It then came to a point where I was holding on to my 9-to-5 and afraid to let go of the comfort of a paycheck. Well, that year in the "Christmas Day" arrival package, John sent me three books: *How to Start, Finance, and Operate Your Own Business*, *The Business of Consulting (The Basics and Beyond)*, and *How to Succeed as an Independent Consultant*. I was so thankful to receive these books and gave them a good glance and placed them in my library.

Months passed and John and I were having another conversation where I was lamenting how I wanted to stop working. He then asked me, "Where are the books I sent you?" I was silent. I knew I had the books but had not read them. I had placed them in the bookcase. He then said to me, "I suggest you pull those books down, read them, and get about setting up your consulting business." And I did. In 1996, I created my consulting business, J Pat Consulting, through which I continue to provide consulting services for organizations designing Diversity, Equity, Inclusion (DEI) initiatives, providing leadership training and conflict resolution, and other human resources solutions. He lit his gentle fire under me, and I am thankful to him for that.

These are just a few of the many ways John touched my life and the lives of others. He was that big brother you could look up to and depend on. He lived his life with flexibility—but very intentional. John was always there not only for me, but for others.

The Later Years

On April 25, 1997, John was featured as guest artist during the 124th Founders' Day Celebration for the University of Arkansas at Pine Bluff. In 1998, John was honored with induction into the Arkansas Jazz Hall of Fame alongside Bob Dorough, Roseanne Vitro, and Art Porter Jr. Unfortunately, he was on tour in Europe and could not attend, so I accepted the award on his behalf. I recall discussing my acceptance speech with him, and he fondly remembered how Art Porter, Sr., gave him his first gig.

As a soloist, John was described by fellow musicians as the "preacher" because of his deeply emotional style. Although his main instrument was tenor saxophone, he was also a respected soprano saxophonist and flutist. He was sought after by traditional jazz, avant-garde, and big band groups throughout his career.

In 2000, W. Royal Stokes wrote *Living the Jazz Life,* a book including conversations he conducted with 40 musicians about their careers in jazz. John was included in the book and once again provided information about his journey as a jazz musician. When Stokes learned I wanted to write a book about John, he said, "John certainly deserves a book, Joyce. I greatly admired his artistry and found him to be a most simpatico cat. He once sent me a postcard from Japan—just to say hello!"

John's final performance in Little Rock was in March 2003 when he was invited by Marguerite Palmer to pay tribute to her son, music critic Robert Palmer, at the University of Arkansas at Little Rock's 75th anniversary celebration. Robert Palmer described John in this way:

In the era of College-produced clones and jazz covers, Stubblefield is the "genuine article"—combining both "his intellect and soul." He is so unique because of his background, which combines a regional Southwest influence including stints in R&B bands as a teenager, as well as a scholarship to a University music course and formal studies with the famous AACM in Chicago. At 50, every aspect of his playing such as his identifiable sound reflects the nature and unique stylist he is. Stubblefield is also one of the strongest jazz composers around.

October 2004 was the last time John would go into the recording studio with the Mingus Band. On that day, he left the hospital and conducted the band from his wheelchair in the recording of three of his arrangements for the album *I Am Three*. Over the years, the Mingus Band has had six Grammy nominations and won a Grammy in 2011.

Our Brother William (BiBi)

This recollection is about our brother William, whom I called BiBi. This is a profound memory for me because it taught me a lot about how we respond during times of grief. John was always an advocate of looking at things on the bright side or from a deeper perspective.

William was extremely talented and could do a lot of things that John and I hadn't a clue. He was an artist, musician, barber, all of which just came natural to him. I remember when William wanted to drive. One day he told Dad, "I can drive that car," and he did. He got in drove and it with little effort, not one lesson. I was very impressed.

William became ill suddenly in February 2001. It caught John and me by total surprise. John was scheduled to be on tour In Osaka, Japan, and I had planned my first trip to Paris. After William became Ill, all of those plans were on hold. This was one of those bittersweet times with John. We both were totally off balance, waiting to see if William was going to make it. Unfortunately, William did not recover from his illness and transitioned on

February 20, 2001. While planning for William's service, John and I had words. Yes, for the first time in years we were at odds with each other. John loved the hymn "Take My Hand, Precious Lord" and he often told me the story about the lyricist Thomas A. Dorsey. As we were preparing the program, I asked John to play this song at the service. He looked and me and told me he couldn't. From my perspective I thought he would be glad to do so since he loved this song so much. After the funeral, we were at odds for a period of time, and of course I was not happy with that. After all, all we had from our biological family now was each other. John went on tour to Japan and upon returning we ironed things out (as he would say). He told me he had written an Elegy to William, and this piece of music had allowed him to truly "let out" the grief he felt with William's transition. He said once he completed this piece of music and it was played, all of his stored grief was released and that was why he just could not play Thomas Dorsey's song at William's service. I felt terrible—now I fully understood why. We agreed we were both grieving and we must continue to move forward. After all, this is what William would want. We vowed never again to let anything come between us—and we didn't.

It was during this time of grief I remember how John often spoke of his journey as a musician. There were times he would call and express his disappointment in where he was in his career. He would tell me he had expected to be much further along. On a few occasions he spoke of walking away from the music; however, I reminded him that was not an option for him and he knew it. You see, music was John's first language, a way of communicating emotions he could never express in words; this is what happened when William transitioned. John could not communicate his grief until he had written the music. He finally expressed his emotions through the music for William, and he was then free to continue moving forward.

Ciao

John celebrated his 60th birthday on February 4, 2005. Sue Mingus threw a surprise birthday party for him at her home. I recall he was fussy that night, but I kept focused on his surprise Birthday Party. You see, our parents and brother William all transitioned in their 50s, and it was my prayer to God that John would see age 60, and he did. That night we all gathered at Sue's—my family, cousins Harry Stubblefield and Stephanie Barber, classmates Charles Smith, Jimmy Davis, and Wendell Jones who flew in from various cities, and the many musicians who came to be with John on his 60th birthday. It was difficult to keep the surprise from John. You know, he had that sixth sense, and during the evening he began to question what was going on. He wanted to know where we were going to dinner, and were we going any other place, etc. Again, I just went with the flow and finally he did too. I will always remember that night and all the love John was given by all. I was so thankful to Sue that John was celebrated in such a special way. This was his last birthday celebration.

Through the years when John and I would part, he never, ever said good bye to me. His parting word was "Ciao."

John first revealed his true illness to me upon his return from his final tour of Europe with the Mingus band in April 2004. We had talked before he left for the tour, and he had expressed that his back was hurting, but I had no idea how ill he was. After talking with him, I called Sue Mingus and asked her what was going on. She replied, "John has acted differently all during the tour. We only see him when he is performing." She also added she had tried to talk with him, but he was distant and had not revealed anything to her. She expressed her concern about John's behavior during the tour, and I told her I was leaving for New York the next day and would be in touch with her. After that, Sue and I stayed in close contact during John's illness and transition.

My first thought was to bring him home to Little Rock. After talking with the social worker, she advised it would not be good to suddenly change his environment—it would be best for John to remain in New York. Following these instructions, John remained in New York and I went to New York to be with him during his illness.

This was a time when I was so afraid. The thought of my brother being ill was just too much for me to handle. Our parents and brother had passed away, and it was just us—John and me. If John transitioned, I would be the only remaining member of our family. I had to be strong and not stay in a place of fear; after all, there was too much to be done, and as soon as those thoughts tried to consumed me, I resolved I was going to do everything I could to make sure I was there for my brother. I was there with my brother making decisions with him until he was no longer able to do so.

In February 2004, he was admitted to Calvary Hospital in Bronx, New York. Dr. Alma Harrington was his oncologist. The care she and her team provided for John was incredible. She was thorough and took the time to explain John's treatments and condition in terms I could clearly understand. John was very involved in his medical care from April 2004 until March of 2005 when the real decline began to show. One of his friends from Jazzmobile, Sarina Bachleitner, kept him stocked with journals. I am thankful for these books because they give a full look into his daily thoughts during his hospitalization.

Sue Mingus's visits were frequent, along with band members and other musicians. Someone was there every day. Those visits were true medicine for John. Over and over I saw the musicians come and spend time with him—and this was not just a few minutes. Many stayed for hours talking about and listening to "the music." John would sit up in his bed, tell jokes, review arrangements, and reminiscent about their times playing and touring together. While they were there, it would appear he was not ill at all. When they left, his pain would return and he had to rest.

John had friends from all walks of life. One I recall who visited frequently and reached out to President Clinton regarding John's illness was Jacquelyn Gallus. One day she came by and told us it was official; plans were being made for President Clinton to visit John at Calvary Hospital. Even though the date and time had not been confirmed, I advised the hospital administration of the impending visit. I do not think they believed me. Finally, they were notified that the Secret Service would visit the hospital. This is when the administration began to act quickly in preparation for that visit. President Clinton visited John on June 15, 2005. He wrote this in John's journal: "I am so glad we got to visit—I loved seeing you and hearing your music too. You're a good man, and an inspiration. God Bless You."

At the time John was ill, the band was working on releasing a new CD, *I Am Three*. John is remembered in this way in the liner notes:

Most notably—for the first time after a dozen years of perform-ing in the Mingus Big Band—John Stubblefield contributed three stunning arrangements, causing us to regret the years we weren't aware of the treasure within our midst. Although John was in the hospital during the recording of this CD and unable to per-form on his saxophone, he arrived in his BATMOBILE—as he calls his wheelchair—to conduct his three arrangements. It was an extraordinary autumn afternoon at Peter Karl's studio in Brooklyn. Music director Alex Foster describes it as one of the most moving, enlightening recording experiences of his life. John Stubblefield talked down all three pieces, gave an overview of Mingus's intentions as he himself understood and interpreted them, and inspired a roomful of musicians to play their hearts out for the next six hours. "No one analyzes music anymore and puts it in historic perspective," Foster said. "It was a masterful way to deal with the music." The three pieces are "Song With Orange"—a blues suite "with a new blues song form" as Stubbs described it—that begins this recording, "Pedal Point Blues" which ends it, and "Orange Is the Color of Her Dress." Of the swinging life he brings to these arrangements, Stubblefield says: "I don't get in Charles Mingus's way. I might add something, a little pepper, a little salt, some cayenne. But I follow his lead. Because you can't interfere with the spirit."

"Pay attention to the shuffle!" Stubblefield shouts from his chair. "It's not a Chicago-style shuffle. It's a NEW ORLEANS-style shuffle!" His eyes flash. "And the dynamics!—does any musician here know anyone who ever managed to play soft besides Eddie Henderson and Chet Baker?" By the end of the day, three great pieces were in the can and Stubbs, grumbling but pleased, headed back in his van sending his good byes to all the cats and all the kittens."

That day was John's last visit to the recording studio.

The Music Lives On

In January, Dr. Carrington began carefully preparing me for what was coming and things to look for. She further stated that John had lasted much longer than most of her patients, but it was time to begin making arrangements. I flew home and made the arrangements and returned quickly to New York.

Again, in April, she counseled me regarding John's declining condition. She advised that things were changing, and John was not able to initiate well but could repeat things said to him. It was during this time that the new CD *I Am Three* was released, and Sue brought copies to the hospital. It was John's desire to autograph my copy. It was difficult, but he did sign it. Yes, I could see things were different, but at this time I knew what was to come—he was just too ill to stay here.

Near the end, John slept a lot, but at points when awake, he was able to say a few things. I recall one night he awakened and said to me, "Joyce, tell me again who my band directors were." I started to name them quickly because I could hear the urgency in his voice—this was important to him. I replied, "Dunbar Junior High School: Leon Adams, Sylvia Clay. Horace Mann: Art Porter, Sr., Allen White. And AM&N College: Harold Strong (Juice Juice Turn Me Loose) and Odie Burrus, Jr." After that, he went back to sleep.

On July 1, 2005, I was watching TV late at night in John's room. I noticed that they continued to flash Luther Vandross on the screen—it did not take long for me to realize Luther had made his transition. I quickly turned the TV down low so John could not hear it. I looked at John as he lay there in his bed and thought, "You are going to make your transition on July 4. After all, that will be going out with a bang."

On July 3, again John was going in and out of sleep and I was in the room sitting with him. His eyes came open and he was just looking straight ahead at the wall. I asked him, "What do you see?"

He responded, "I see people."

I asked him, "Who are the people? Do you see Mom, Dad, William?"

He responded again, "I see people".

My next question was, "Do you know who I am?"

He responded clearly, "You are my Sister for Life." I will never forget that moment. I cried silently and privately because I did not want him to know I was crying. This reply from my brother is with me each day. After all, I am his "Sister for Life."

On the evening of July 4, 2005, about 7:00 p.m., our cousins Harry Stubblefield and Stephanie Barber, a few friends, and I had the privilege of being with John during his last moments. The room was filled with a sense of peace and serenity as he transitioned . As his transition was confirmed by the doctor, I looked out the seventh-floor window of Calvary Hospital in the Bronx, and I saw a huge explosion of fireworks in the sky. The colors were fantastic, and the atmosphere for some was that of celebration; however, for us grief. Yes, John, transitioned with a celebration like no other. The jazz world had lost one of its brightest stars. You see, my brother was not just a musician, he was a maestro. I remember the first time I heard him play; he played from his soul, and his long fingers would wrap around those notes painting a sound that lingered in the air long after he had stopped playing.

As the fireworks exploded, I cried and said Ciao to my amazing brother and thanked God for making me his "Sister for Life." As I said goodbye to John, I will always remember the joy he brought through his music and the determined spirit that defined his life. His legacy will forever echo through the melodies he created and the lives he touched.

We held a private burial for John in Little Rock on July 15, 2005, and a memorial service was held the next day at Greater Center Star Baptist Church. John was survived by his son, John C. Stubblefield, and me. His granddaughter, Halie Stubblefield, was born in January 2010.

John was posthumously inducted into the Arkansas Black Hall of Fame in October 2007. The John Stubblefield Papers reside in the Special Collections Library at the University of Arkansas at Fayetteville. Recently, five two-track masters of unreleased music by the Charles Mingus Quintet were discovered. These recordings were done on February 13, 1973, in Detroit, Michigan, at an event called Jazz in Detroit. John was one of the five members of the quintet at the time. One writer said John's "bubbly tenor covers the spectrum from blues shouts to sleek post-bop lines." This was a historic performance that lasted for over three hours. The discovery of this music is welcomed by all. It is powerful music for many to relive and others to enjoy for the first time. Both CDs and albums were released in November 2018.

John loved music so much and enjoyed performing, writing, and creating it. He devoted his life to being the best he could be. He was a giver. His love for music and life and his dedication to "the music" was always magical. He shared his love for music with the world, inspiring countless musicians and captivating audiences in dimly lit clubs and grand concert halls. John knew that music had the power to heal and unite, and through his compositions, he touched the hearts of many. As I savor the electrifying memories of my brother's performances over the years, I find solace in the fact that his music continues to touch my life. This connection became remarkably clear on my birthday in 2021.

Celebrating at 42 Restaurant in the Clinton Library in Little Rock, I navigated pandemic protocols, and as I entered the building, I heard a familiar song, "Sentimental Mood" by Duke Ellington and John Coltrane. This was a tune I knew well; it was one of John's favorites, often played during his visits home and during performances. As I listened, I sensed it was my brother playing. Despite the Covid protocols, I was determined to get to the gift shop to confirm who was playing—I already knew! You see, this song began playing the moment I stepped inside the building, and the last notes played as I signed in. In haste, I rushed to the gift shop to identify who was playing this music. Just as I thought, the CD label read: John Stubblefield "Sentimental Mood." The odds of this occurrence were slim, but I choose to believe that John's spirit was present, celebrating my birthday. Thanks, big brother!

John was a man of faith who embraced life to its fullest. This was evident in a note I discovered in his horn case upon his return from his final European tour: "I know the Lord, he'll make a way."

Ciao

Do as much as you can do
with the time that you have
in the place where you are.

— Ramon Daniel Espino

VII. Influencers

Starting with his parents and his early exposure to music in church, John's journey unfolded through encounters with figures like Rosetta Tharpe, Mrs. Rice his fourth-grade teacher who suggested he have piano lessons, and Mrs. Douglas his piano teacher who laid the foundation for his musical prowess. The foundation Mrs. Douglas built for John in reading, writing, and playing music was solid, and he carried that knowledge into his professional life. A pivotal moment occurred with the friendship with John Bush, connecting him to saxophonist Don Byas. Then came his music directors—Leon Adams and Sylvia Clay in junior high school, Art Porter, Sr., and Allen White in senior high, and Harold Strong and Odie Burrus, Jr., at AM&N College, along with York Wilbourn with whom he made his first recording, and many other local musicians.

John's musical journey extended beyond college, immersing him in the influences of renowned legendary musicians as Nat Adderley, Louis Armstrong, Sil Austin, Kenny Baron, Count Basie, Art Blakey, Buddy Bolden, Dave Brubeck, Don Byas, Hank Crawford, Ornette Coleman, John Coltrane, Hank Crawford, Miles Davis, Duke Ellington, Gil Evans, Dexter Gordon, Dizzy Gillespie, Herbie Hancock, Coleman Hawkins, Jimmy Heath, Joe Henderson, Freddie Hubbard, Abdullah Ibrahim, Roland Kirk, Melba Liston, Charles Mingus, Thelonious Monk, Jelly Roll Morton, Amina-Claudine Myers, Charlie Parker, Tito Puente, Sam Rivers, Sonny Rollins,

George Russell, Pharoah Sanders, Wayne Shorter, Horace Silver, Jimmy Smith, William Grant Still, McCoy Tyner, Stanley Turrentine, Mary Lou Williams, Lester Young, and countless others. This roster represents just a fraction of the musicians John often spoke about, sharing his deep passion for learning, which continued throughout his professional life. After college, John went on to Chicago, spending many hours associating with the AACM and influential musicians like Muhal Abrams, Joseph Jarman, Maurice McIntyre, and Henry Threadgill, Kenny Barron, Jr. Parker, and others. In an interview concerning the AACM, John remarked, "I could write and hear the music I wrote weekly. Later I could write for the personalities of the people who were in the band. I knew the strong parts; I knew the weak parts, and that was something that I always wanted to do. The AACM was exactly what I needed at that time."

After moving to New York, John met Charles Mingus, whose collaboration left a lasting impact. Mingus's influences were significant, and even after parting ways early in John's career, their paths crossed again in the 90s. Mary Lou Williams, the first person to hire John in New York, played a crucial role in John's life, and one of their collaborations resulted in a song entitled "Baby Man," which was written at the time John's son was born.

There were many who contributed to John's musical tapestry, enabling him to become a brave innovator who fearlessly transcended the confines of traditional jazz. His unique approach involved blending genres and pushing boundaries, redefining jazz and music as he envisioned in his head and heart. John's legacy lies in being a musician's musician, admired for his bold and groundbreaking contributions to the world of music.

Photo Album

The Stubblefield family, May 1967: (seated) Johnnie C. and Mable Stubblefield;
(standing) John, me, and William

Mom and Dad on Easter Sunday, March 30, 1975

John and his son, John C.—the next generation

John graduated from Horace Mann High School in May 1963 where he was a member of the Student Council and served as Sergeant-at-Arms.

In May 1967, John graduated from Arkansas Mechanical and Normal College (AM&N, aka "The Yard") where he was active in both the marching and concert bands.

The Zenith Center where John watched, heard, and played music

John in the band room at AM&N College practicing with his soprano saxophone in 1964

John performing with his primary horn, the tenor saxophone

John performing with the Concert Band while attending AM&N College

John surrounded himself with "the music," taking every opportunity to play whether in college or in other venues.

John's band the New Directions Quintet: (from left) John, James Leary, Sonelius Smith, Benjamin Jones, and Larry Ross.

This photo was used on the cover of John's first album, Prelude, *released in 1976.*

JOHN STUBBLEFIELD

JOHN STUBBLEFIELD
JOHN STUBBLEFIELD
PHOTO BY:
JIMMY KATZ

John (far right) with the Mingus Band

John at a recording session in New York City with Sue Mingus in the background

A quick photo op on the road: Alex Sipiagin, Sue Mingus, John Hicks, and John in Stockholm to perform at the Sweden Jazz Festival in 2001

The Mingus Big Band performing with John on the far right wearing one of his favorite hats

Members of the Mingus Big Band at Clinton Recording Studios, March 2, 1993.
Seated on floor, left to right: *Kenny Drew, Jr., Craig Handy, Joe Locke.* Standing, left to
right, first row: *Producer Sue Mingus, John Stubblefield, Alex Foster, Marvin "Smitty"
Smith, Jack Walrath, Sam Burtis, and Dave Taylor.* Standing, left to right, back row:
*Frank Kuumba Lacy, Ray Mantilla, Michael Formanek, Steve Slagle, Andy McKee, Randy
Brecker, Ryan Kisor, Ronnie Cuber, Chris Kase, and Chris Potter. (Photo by Jimmy
Katz/Giant Steps)*

John onstage in Paris

One of my many postcards from John

John Sent
Postcards
from Around
the Globe:

Africa

Amsterdam

Asia

Australia

Austria

England

Finland

France

Germany

Greece

India

Italy

Japan

Norway

Portugal

Russia

Turkey

John (fourth from left) with the Fort Apache Band

John (left) with the Michelle Rosewoman Band on a three-week tour of Europe in 1984

*John, Albert Sun, and Frank Kuumba Lacy at the Aix-en-Provence, France,
Outdoor Festival, July 2002*

*Some of John's memorabilia (hats and album covers) on display at the University
of Arkansas at Fayetteville, July 2010*

John and me on my whirlwind trip to New York in 1994

John and me and my pink satin baby outfit from "The Birthday Story"

John and his horns

John plays solo using the circular breathing technique.

Poster for a concert to honor John at the University of Arkansas at Fayetteville.

"The music" was always on John's mind.

The Interviews

As I stated earlier, I began writing the initial pages of this book in July 2005. Wrestling with the pain of John's absence, I wrote several pages to capture memories and maintain perspective. However, the weight of grief led me to place this project on the shelf for several years.

This book now unfolds as a narrative shaped by some of my personal recollections of my brother. Over time, I realized that the insights and memories shared by his musical family and friends were equally important. Organized alphabetically, the following remembrances stem from interviews I conducted with them. I am deeply grateful for their willingness to share their memories and to collaborate on this endeavor.

John and I met when he first came to New York. He had just arrived and was living on St. Felix Street near the Brooklyn Academy of Music. Several great musicians lived on that street—Gary Bartz, Betty Carter, Hubert Eaves, Stafford James—yes, this street was full of musicians! John's first gig was playing for a dance at the Audubon Ballroom, and that is actually where we met.

Like all of us, John played gigs to make a living. He excelled and worked with the key musicians in New York. I know he played with Nat Adderley, Mingus, and the Fort Apache Band and several others. John and I would visit for hours. We enjoyed cooking (chicken or fish) and talking about music. There were times we would talk so much we would forget we were cooking. A lot of our talks were about deep stuff like religion and philosophy.

John was a great musician. He was one of those guys whose talent should certainly have been recognized; however, John in many ways was an unsung hero. Like many of the musicians of that period, John was involved in the making and transition of Black music during the 60s and through the 80s. It was during this period that the music began to be identified for Black people. Also, during this time many Black musicians were starting their own record companies because they wanted to be in control of their music.

John was recognized, but not nearly as much as he should have been. He was persistent in his pursuit of music. He studied, taught, played music from all aspects. His focus was on the spiritual and technical aspects of music.

I recall when we were playing at the Audubon Ballroom, people were dancing and having a good time. There was a lady there who danced so hard her wig flew off her head. She was so engrossed in the music that her wig could not stay on.

I want the world to remember John's personality. He was a man who knew what he wanted to do and he did it. He had a friendly, warm personality and his persistence as a musician was powerful. He was always professional, and he never slacked on the job. John Stubblefield gave his full self to the music.

Lee Anthony

I first met John Stubblefield while attending AM&N College. I was ahead of John there. I first started listening to John's music when he was with a group called the Tasty Bag Full (John, Thomas East, Sonelius Smith, and Dewitt Chapel, aka David I.). I recorded his group, The New Directions, in the mid 60s. John's group participated in the National Collegiate Jazz Festival in Indiana and won the competition, which launched their first European tour.

When they got home from that trip, I recorded the group in my studio (Soul Brother Recording Studio) in Little Rock. I was the first to do a demo on The New Directions in my studio. This all happened the year that I graduated from AM&N College. I also recorded The New Directions when they returned to AM&N College, which had become the University of Arkansas at Pine Bluff, for a 10-year reunion.

In our last conversation, John and I talked about the early music, recordings. I have always been fascinated with music and especially recording music. I recall while in school, my teacher Mr. Strong brought in a tape recorder and allowed each student to speak into it. I have never forgotten that day when I heard my voice on that recorder!

My first recording was done with a home machine that I pulled around in a wagon where I set up my own speakers and mic. I would bring my recorder to the student union building and do various recordings while there. I basically recorded anyone who wanted to be recorded, and that included John's group when they were performing. I pawned my class ring to buy a voice recorder and old juke boxes to increase the sound of my recordings. I purchased four juke boxes and used three of them to create a base amplifier. This really upgraded my sound and recording ability. I still have that equipment.

My first impression of John was he was a very serious musician from the beginning. He was way ahead of his time. He did not pull any punches; his ego was not bigger than his talent. John was always an even spirit to me. He did not have to prove nothing to anyone. He did what musician do—he came out and played. John had a lot of talent. I just know the group was good!

As a musician, John stood out. I did not know that many horn players; however, John and Dewitt Chapel (David I.) stood out. John was different. I did not know what was going to happen with John—but I knew *something* was going to happen.

I would like the world to remember that John Stubblefield was a real nice guy. Never knew him to be nothing but even spirited. He was dedicated to his talent and was a perfect gentleman. He came from a small city where a lot of people's talent went unknown. Little Rock did not know what to do with good musicians like John—York Wilburn, Art Porter, Henry Shead, Pharoah Sanders, Dewitt Chapel, and many others. We never got over the "57 syndrome" and it still hoovers over the city. In spite of it all, John continued to move forward and play the music he loved.

Sarina Bachleitner

I first met John when I was 16 years old. I had decided at age 13 that I wanted to be a jazz musician, and I spent a lifetime pursuing that passion and maintaining a full-time career in the jazz idiom. When I was 16, jazz was not in the educational arena, so I was turning over every stone to find like-minded musicians who could mentor me toward my dream. I heard about the Jazzmobile up in Harlem and was told it was the place to be. When I arrived there, I was met by John Stubblefield, who was the director of the program. He readily asked me to audition for him and I played him a song I had transcribed. (Back then we actually transcribed music to learn instead of buying the sheet music.)

The song was "Round Midnight" by Thelonious Monk. I was proud that I had also transcribed some of his solo and reflected that in my audition. When I had finished playing, John said, "Wow, you sound just like Monk. But what about you?" So I readily played a song I had written that seemed less than adequate, but well received. John took the time to speak with me for what was close to an hour and then asked if I wanted to sit in on the big band. I had never played in an ensemble before and was terrified. However, I was pretty tenacious at that age and determined to get my experiences where I could.

Here was a 16-piece big band, fully equipped with the highest caliber of NYC musicians, and all I knew was my D dorian mode. So John proudly announced my participation, and a daunting piece of music was placed before me. My stomach fell. It had chord symbols and complex meters all over the page—but the music had started, and I just fell in. Along came the piano solo, and I did the pedantic eight-note sloppy feel that all amateurs do within the realm of the D dorian mode (which clearly didn't belong) and, with an out-of-body experience, knew I had completely failed and ruined the music.

When the music came to a close, I eyeballed the nearest exit in hopes of leaving the scene of the crime as soon as possible. Yet I met with what I eventually learned to be the epitome of the jazz community spirit. I was congratulated on my performance. I was embraced with accolades of praise for my courage and natural instinct for jazz and encouraged to pursue my dream.

At the close of an inspiring day, John walked me to the bus stop, and we talked for several hours, exchanged phone numbers, and promised to reunite again. When I got home, I am sure my mom got an earful. I remember telling her that someday I would start a jazz program just like the Jazzmobile but for younger students like myself. As it turned out, John became my mentor for the next 25 years.

Mentorship

Throughout the years, I received many invitations from John to attend his concerts, educational sessions, and frequent late-night diner hangs after a gig. Whenever I was invited to a gig, John always brought me backstage to introduce me to every musician. He always introduced me as a wonderful pianist and composer as if he was a proud dad bragging about his daughter. John knew that my dad had left when I was very young and that he had been an aspiring jazz musician. Somehow, my only connection to my biological dad was our love for jazz. John knew the significance of this and took on a paternal role throughout my life.

I remember the days when he would take me kite flying in Central Park and Battery Street Park and I would tease him about the fact that for all of our efforts, the kite never took flight. Yet those moments of kite flying were the closest and most valuable feelings of normal family life that I had ever experienced. Somehow, those moments meant more to me than the music, because it filled a lonely void in my heart.

There were times I wanted to quit playing jazz because as a young white female, I was a minority in the field and not yet strong enough a player to compete in a man's world. Yet John always said, "You cannot quit, because the music is a part of you." And so I kept on. As the years passed, my mantra for success was "take any gig—with anyone, anywhere, anytime, for any money." As a result I became a versatile player and educator that circulated in the blues, jazz, and pop arena.

I was quite savvy in the art of booking gigs, so I developed my own jazz quintet, an R&B band called Shaketown, started the Jazz Apprenticeship Program, and managed to maintain a viable career in music. Through it all, John was always present. When I started the Jazz Apprenticeship Program in 1997, Slide Hampton and John were my first hires for the foundling program.

One day, John and I sat at our favorite diner and reminisced about our lifetime friendship. He remembered the promise I had made back in 1980, when I promised to someday run my own jazz program. In 2011, the program had moved to Jazz at Lincoln Center and our final concert attributed much of its music to compositions written by the late, great John Stubblefield.

Carroll Baikida

My memories of John are of a gracious man who made anyone in his presence feel as though they were the paramount person on the planet. He was a true gentlemen and always attentive to the needs of others. We performed in quite a few bands together, including Oliver Lake and Michele Rosewoman. He had agreed to join my band and record on my album *Door of the Cage*, but the logistics didn't work out.

My fondest memories of him are of exploring the Rijksmuseum in Amsterdam and riding around NYC in a van for what seemed like hours, telling jokes and philosophizing, while frantically looking for a good restaurant at 3:00 in the morning after a gig at Sweet Basil's.

Besides, all of our personal interactions, John was a powerful master musician and a true artist!

I miss him dearly!

Kenny Barron

I met John in Chicago at Ahmad Jamal's club. While there, John asked me about some chords in one of my songs, so this is how we met. Later he moved to New York and we would talk and laugh about that first meeting. He was a very unassuming, nice guy.

When I first heard John play in New York, he had an incredible sound. He told me he had spent time playing with Solomon Burke. Eventually I started my band and I gave John a call. He had this magical way of playing, a very strong and creative player. That was it for me. John was well loved and respected.

I remember when John would play, he would take very long solos. He loved to play, and I loved it. Once, we were playing in New York, and in a one-hour set we only played three songs. This happened because everyone started playing long solos. John made it interesting by doing this, and most people did not notice that only three songs were played.

I cannot think of anything unusual other than that John was very cool. We got to travel to Europe a couple of times, and we also went to India. That was big fun. There was a big jazz festival in Bombay, India. John was very curious about the music in India and wanted to know more about it.

I would like for the world to remember that John was a great player, a great composer. In fact, I recorded several of his compositions. He was very serious about music and he had a wide palette—and he was a really sweet cat.

Years after attending a Quincy Troupe performance in Brooklyn, I was crossing Houston Street. A gentleman approached me from behind. "Did you see Quincy Troupe in Brooklyn? You were a VISION as you walked through the door." I laughingly told myself this guy is a keeper.

I crossed Houston Street often. I was friendly with the Thirteenth Street squatters. I had friends in Tompkins Square. I rehearsed at the University of the Streets with Barry Harris.

John would again approach me on Houston Street. "Would you like to see Eddie Henderson at Sweet Basil's?

Heck, I was a vision. How could I say no?

John and I became fast friends. He was bright, articulate, and had a special way of looking at the world. He loved music but not so much the business. He had definite political opinions and was interested in what I knew medically. We shared the same mind.

John wanted a certain political book. I purchased it and left it at one of his gigs with Michael Carvin, as a surprise.

John was funny. I called him one day. He said he could not talk—Baby and Sugar, his horns, needed attention. They would squawk if they did not get proper attention.

We would meet in Tompkins Square and talk well into the night. He would walk me to Grand Street and I would walk him back to Houston. This back and forth would go on all night.

I surprised him on Valentine's Day with a heart shaped balloon. I called John to his stoop. Surprised, he ran upstairs and brought down a huge heart-shaped box of chocolates. Mind you, we were not romantically involved and he had no idea that I was coming. I sort of guessed that he had an endless supply of Valentine hearts. To this day, I cannot see a large Valentine and not think of John.

John was a session musician at Stax Records. He called me to tell me he had lunch with Isaac Hayes. Hayes worked at Kiss radio at 395 Hudson Street. I worked at 345 Hudson Street. I admonished John, "You had lunch with Isaac Hayes so close and you didn't call ME?" John laughed.

John sent beautiful postcards from around the world. He never forgot me. One particularly beautiful card was of John Coltrane.

John needed a doctor. He wouldn't tell me why. I referred him to a low-cost clinic. Onstage at Fat Cat one night, he ran offstage. When I asked him what was wrong, he said, "Bathroom."

Joyce, his sister, told me John loved me. There are a few people in life that implant in your heart in a special way. I call them "Joys." John Stubblefield was a joy in my life and when I cross over, if he is there, I will surely reach for him.

Melrita Russ Bonner

Our mothers met at the doctor's office when they were pregnant. They started talking and became close friends. I was born on January 30, 1945, and John on February 4, 1945. From that time, our mothers kept visiting one another, and when they visited each other's home they would put us together in the same crib. John and I had a joke where he said I was his first "Hanging Buddy." We slept together first. We grew up together, but we attended separate elementary schools. I went to Bush Elementary School and John to Booker T. Washington Elementary School. We reconnected when we entered Dunbar Junior High.

We always stayed in touch. When I went off to Spelman for college, we always kept in contact. After I got married and moved to Detroit, whenever he performed there, he would get in touch with us and stop by for a visit. John called me his "Spiritual Sister." I loved his energy. I thought he was a very enterprising and caring person. And as a musician, oh, wow, he was off the charts, out of this world. I knew the full background of his musical journey—and how he rose to such great heights.

One memory that stands out to me was when he was visiting with us once in Detroit. John came over and brought some other friends with him. We were all hanging out in our basement listening to music. It was always exhilarating to see him perform in person and think of the connection we had.

When John traveled, we always kept in touch through cards and correspondence. When he came home, he would come to visit, and I would go to see him perform. He would also come home sometimes for our class reunions—Horace Mann Class of 1963. I was there when John performed at the University of Arkansas at Little Rock in 2003. That was his last performance at home—and that was the last time I saw him. Wherever he went, we stayed in touch. Sometimes we would talk on the phone, and he would tell me what he was doing. Periodically, he would send me his albums, CDs, and postcards from around the world. I saw some of his postcards recently, and they were very decorative and pretty and touching.

To me, John was a very gifted, special, and unforgettable person and friend.

Randy Brecker

Simply put, John Stubblefield was the Heart and Soul of the Mingus Big Band. His saxophone playing, especially on "Hog Callin' Blues," made it seem like Mingus wrote the tune and concept for Stubbs himself, even though it was written before Mingus knew of John. The way in which he built that solo was the high point of the night. Every night. In many ways I thought of him as our "fearless leader." On the Band Bus he would sit on his throne the middle of five seats in the last row and shout out to his disciples: "Men! We are men of Testicular Fortitude!" "Barkeeper!" (To the roadie) "Some libation for my Men!"

On one long trip from the airport to a gig a couple hundred miles away, Michel Petrucciani had arrived before us and taken *our* bus, which apparently was much nicer than the one allotted to him. We assembled on the more dilapidated bus, and Stubbs found his throne on the back row and began a diatribe: "That blob is traveling alone. We are over 20 fold, and moreover men of Testicular Fortitude.... That blob didn't have to take our bus! I remember meeting him first time on the bandstand with Freddie Hubbard. Freddie looked at me and I looked at Freddie, and we said to each other: 'We've got to stomp that Momfucker!'"

"Beware of the Blob" became the slogan for the rest of the tour.

I must add at this time that we all had abiding respect and admiration for Michel and his challenges with osteogenesis imperfecta, more often known as glass bones disease. This included John of course, but this was his way of assembling his "troops" and adding dark humor to a difficult situation. That was part or his leadership.

Other times he was the band spokesperson, like when we were performing in France on French Independence Day, and he improvised a long and coherent speech about "Bastille Day" (one and the same day). He knew the history, and with just a minute's notice, he went out and gave an amazing speech.

I have to mention another crazy memory. Maybe it was the early 90s and was billed as a "Tribute to John Coltrane." We went to Japan for an extended tour of the Blue Note Clubs, with Kenny Barron, Gary Bartz, Reggie Workman, and Ralph Peterson. We were all hangin' pretty hard after the gigs. We were young and having a lot of fun. One night after the gig at the Blue Note in Fukuoca, some of us went to the local jazz club there and sat in, and the drinks were flowing. Stubbs and I were maybe the last of the cats there, but I got pretty wasted, and I left John at the piano singin' the blues with some local cats backing him up. A young Japanese drummer named "Chestnut" took me to the hotel and promised to go back and get John.

Well at around 5:30 a.m., the phone rings. I'm in a hung-over deep sleep and it's Chestnut. "Mr. Randy Brecker, I am so sorry to bother you, but I have Mr. John Stubblefield stuck in my car!" I put on slippers and a bathrobe and went outside. Sure enough in this small Japanese car with two hotel employees trying to help, there is Stubbs—not *in* the back seat but face down in the space where your feet touch the floor, snoring loudly, but OUT! It took like an hour to figure out how to remove the two back seats so the four of us could lift Stubbs into a wheelchair and back to his room. In the morning he was dressed like a movie star, totally chipper, and didn't remember a thing. The rest of us had headaches and could barely get out of bed. Testicular fortitude indeed!

When John was taken ill, the Mingus Band had to face an uncertain future without him, but he handled his illness with courage and grace, and was creative until the end. He brought in four great new arrangements to a rehearsal, and we played them at the gig that night.

It's not everyone who can boast about Bill Clinton visiting him in the hospital, but John affected everyone who met him the same way. We all loved and were moved by a special person who was full of music, passion, humor, and love of life. We miss him always with such fond, wonderful, and unique memories.

Cecil Bridgewater

We met at a Collegiate Jazz Festival in St Louis in 1969. I believe he was with his quartet, and I was there with the University of Illinois Big Band. He impressed me as a serious person—he was very serious. He liked Wayne Shorter, and this is how he initially modeled his playing. Later, after getting to New York, he changed. Again, my first impression of John was that he was a serious person and a serious musician.

I recorded an album with him, and he recorded one of my tunes on it. John was very into developing an idea—playing wise. He was developing his style of playing and trying to get as close to that as he could.

He and I played together in James Jabo Ware's Big Band. John wrote a tune we had recorded. I recall during the first take, I did not feel we had gotten to the core of what he wanted. The second take was a much better version of the tune. We went with it. It was emotional to me, and if I did not get the right feeling, I could not go with it, but again, that time was right.

When he came to visit me before his son was born, he kept saying, "My wife is with child." To hear it said that way was old school. John talked about being from the same city where Pharoah Sanders was from, and this made a connection for me regarding the things he was thinking about and the manner in which he spoke.

I recall when John moved to New York. When we lived in Long Island, he and his wife Sharon came out to visit. It was a very pleasant visit. We had children who are close in age—John a son, and I a daughter.

We played at a club in New York. We recorded two albums with Joe Chambers, and we played a lot of John's tunes. We recorded "Blood Count," the last composition by Billy Strayhorn, which was written in the hospital just before Strayhorn died.

During the years, we worked together on some gigs and recorded together, shortly after we disappeared from each other but reunited in Jabo Ware's big band. We were close but we were not playing together. John got sick, and I went by the hospital to visit him. He showed me a book that many musicians who had visited had signed.

I would want the world to realize all of his work and the people he influenced. It is difficult to say one thing. Just to know John was a great joy. He could be an inspiration to anyone who is coming along now. It would be good for the world to know John more than just a name on a record—to get into really knowing him.

Abraham Burton

The first time I remember seeing John I was about 13 years old. I lived down the block not far from the club Sweet Basil. Me and two other friends from the neighborhood would hang out around the club helping musicians set up and would make a few dollars. Having the opportunity to be around these musicians connected us to the music. Mind you I did not met John personally at this point, but he was playing at Sweet Basil with a small group. Because we were under age, they would not let us in the club, so we watched from outside. When John put the horn in his mouth, I remember being blown away. I was standing watching him through the window. I said to the doorman, "Steve, who is that?" and he replied John Stubblefield, one of the greatest players of all time.

The first time I actually spoke to John was at Carlos One on Sixth Avenue. John was playing there, and once again because we were under age, we stood outside the club watching from afar. John did not sound like other players. He played different—I was drawn to his sound. He had so much command when he played, he knew how to build his solos. At the break, I decided to wait outside and talk to him. This was the first time I met John Stubblefield.

John was easy to talk to. He made it comfortable and inviting to be around him. He joked and made us laugh. He saw that we were really young to be following the music in such an intense way. Back then, if a musician saw you were young and interested in "the music," they embraced you as John did us. He made me feel extremely comfortable. He asked me what instrument I played, who I was listening to, and he was genuinely supportive. This was a beautiful experience, a memorable experience.

John was a powerful musician, very powerful when he played. The word that comes to me when describing John's playing is "command." John commanded the music, and he knew it. He knew how to "get you," and he "had you" when he played.

I did not get to know him as an arranger until I started to play in the Mingus Band. My whole relationship with the Mingus Band was initiated by John. Yes, John Stubblefield was 100% responsible for me getting connected with the band. This started around 1993 or '94. At the time I was playing in Art Taylor's Band. Back then, If you were a young musician playing with a master musician, you remained loyal to that group. You did not hop around from band to band. I was asked to join several different groups as well, but I turned the offers down. I was playing with Art Taylor. Still, behind the scenes, John told Sue Mingus about me.

One day Sue called and said she had heard about me through John. Mind you, I had not seen John in a while. I had no idea John Stubblefield knew who I was. He must have heard me with Art Taylor's band or something. She then told me that John had recommended me for the Mingus Band. But I did not join the Mingus band at that time because I was still with Arthur Taylor's group. It was not until 1995 or 1996 after Arthur Taylor passed away that I connected with the Mingus Band.

I think it was 1996 when John called me one day and started talking to me as if we had been communicating with each other for years, or as if we talked daily and we were just picking up the conversation from where we last left off. In that conversation, he told me, "Look, man, I know that Arthur Taylor has passed on. We all loved him very much, but now it is time for you to do something different, and I think this would be a good move for you and the Mingus band. You'll fit right in."

I guess I was surprised that John remembered me because we had only played together once on a short tour with drummer Billy Hart on the West Coast earlier that year. In any case John set the whole thing up during that conversation. He told me to bring my horn down to the club. I said "cool" and did just that. If it were not for John, I might never have been in the Mingus Band. It was not until I joined the Mingus Band that I was introduced to John's ability to write and arrange music.

I can remember while on the road in Europe (Italy or France) we were driving from one city to another. We were all talking, telling jokes, laughing while traveling. John was laughing and joking with us, too, but while he was continuously engaging with us, I noticed he was writing, so I asked him, "What are you writing?"

He replied, "I am arranging a piece for the big band." I thought to myself, he is arranging a piece for the big band? While riding on the bus, talking, laughing, and joking with us, without the use of a piano or at least his sax? That blew me away! I was really blown away when we played the arrangement. I could not believe John was writing these arrangements without any reference other than what he was hearing in his head. John was not only a great player; he was a well-rounded musician. John was bad! He wrote and arranged with the same passion he played, and he breathed the same passion into people who knew him.

We were always watching John. He was the centerpiece of that big band. He was "the cat." A beautiful lesson for me, and a real turning point as a musician, occurred one night when I was still young and feeling good about how I was playing on this particular night. I played a few solos with the big band, and the audience responded favorably. That was important to the younger cats, and John understood that because we were up and coming musicians. There was another young sax player who was getting a lot of attention that night along with me. Needless to say we were defi-nitely "feeling ourselves."

On this particular night while we were getting a lot of atten-tion, John sat in his chair, relaxed, working on his reeds as usual. He frequently worked on his reeds, shaving them down and mark-ing them for respective instruments. John was very meticulous with reeds. He had different types of instruments for which he shaved and smoothed out the reeds. This was his routine. He was very involved in getting them just right—this mattered to him that much. In the meanwhile, we were playing all the solos and feeling good about ourselves, I recall the song was "Peggy's Blue Skylight." We whispered to John, "Why don't you play on this one?" John nodded and said no, you go ahead and play.

Well, I guessed we thought that John was intimidated to play after us, so we kept bugging him. First, he said he did not have his glasses, and we pointed out that his glasses were on his neck con-nected to eyeglass straps. When we asked again, he responded, "I do not have the chord changes." Now confident that even the great John Stubblefield was afraid to play after us, we arrogantly passed the chord changes to John. It was just about time for the next solo.

John stood up with his tenor, leaving his glasses dangling around his neck from his eyeglass strap. I thought to myself, "How is he going to read the music?" He began what would turn out to be the most captivating and perfect solo that night. That solo had every element of the music necessary. He started slow, with long lyr-ical melodies and phrases. His tone was rich and full. He showcased the usage of space, vocabulary, phrasing—and the building of the solo was unbelievable. I remember watching him. He wasn't looking at any music. He was just blowing, playing from his heart, bringing everything to a boil, and then a beautiful peaceful cadence.

I looked at the other sax player next to me and his mouth was open, and that's when I realized my mouth was open, too. As soon as John finished, the crowd went wild. He quietly passed the music back to us, sat down, put his glasses back on, and went back to shaving his reeds.

John and I never spoke a word about that night. We did not have to. It was a spanking well deserved. It made us realize there was a pecking order, and he did it with grace and dignity toward us. John was really supportive by letting us play most of the solos to help boost our confidence, notoriety, and experience, but that night John gently schooled us in respect for musicians, especially our elders. It was a beautiful night.

He was a very special man both on and off the bandstand, very caring. He was a character. He could make you laugh and think deeply about something. I remember the last time I went to see him at Calvary Hospital. As I walked into the room, I was his only visitor. He called to me and said to come quick. There was a CD playing, and he told me to put the CD back. When it started to play, I realized it was an album we did with the Mingus Big Band. It was my solo. He told me, "Listen, listen, you hear that?"

I said, "What, John?" He then told me to put the CD back again. When it started to play again, I realized he was referring to the space I was leaving in between my phrases.

He said again, "You hear that, the space? Now you are really getting it. You are growing and maturing." Can you imagine? Even while ill, John was still listening so deeply to the important intricacies of the music, my music. John was still teaching. He never stopped.

John was a sweetheart. He had a special gift. He knew how to engage with others. He knew how to make others feel appreciated. He was selfless. He was an amazing man.

John Bush

I first met John Stubblefield (Stub) in junior high school in Little Rock in the seventh grade. My friend Mahlon Martin and John registered for band the first semester of school, but I didn't. (Back then you had to register in the summer for first-semester classes.) I wanted to be in the band, though, so I got in the second semester.

My first impression of Stub was I knew he was all right. He had to be cool. I really liked him. He played in the band. We didn't know it at first, but we were both friends with Mahlon Martin. I had met Mahlon in kindergarten, and our grandfathers were strong church buddies in the AME church. Our families knew each other well. Stub and Mahlon knew each other from living in the South End. From my perspective if Mahlon knew Stub, Stub was cool.

Without a question Stub could play. He was my whole point for wanting to play in the band. One does not think of Stub, you just live it. As teenagers, we did not think about Stub in ranking acquaintances. It was just natural love. It is like air when it is taken for granted. Language does not lend itself to describing feelings. You just take time to identify it. You just experience it. This is how I saw Stub.

I remember Mrs. Hegwood, our homeroom teacher, kicking me out of class. I was sitting there talking to Stub during homeroom, and she—having strong theatrical and dramatic tendencies about everything—went into action. Everything to her was about theatre and drama. Stub and I were whispering and talking, and she freaked out from her desk. "Aweee I told you boys," (while clutching her pearls with a hand over her head) "you will need to leave the room." She put me, not Stub, out of homeroom, and I had to go to the principal's office and could not return without my parents. The next day my father took me back to school. I was just as straight as they came, but I got in trouble and Stub did not. It was so embarrassing having to bring my father back to school, but she did not really remember why I was kicked out of school. Stub got away clean and I did not.

We used to go on band trips. I learned to play flute. I was always the biggest dude in the band, and yeah, I learned to play flute. I remember Brenda Evans and I were the two flute players. They used to tease me about it. It was during this time Stub would not take the tenor out of his mouth on the hottest days of the year in the marching band. There was no one who played in the band who did not know Stub. Mr. Adams, Mrs. Clay, all of the band directors liked him. They recognized that Stub was the Man in the Band.

It is ironic that Stub had the opportunity to meet my uncle, Don Byas who was known as one of the greatest of all tenor players. Don was originally from Muskogee, Oklahoma, and he was married to my father's sister. My aunt passed away, and he continued his career in Europe for over 20 years making periodic trips back to the U.S.

I recall introducing Stub to my adopted brother, Gary Hammon. Actually, I made two introductions. The other was to my friend Booker T. Williams. Stub did make the connections, and they became good friends. He liked them just as I did.

Stub was a good man. He was not selfish. He was never selfish with the music. He was that kind of jazz musician. He loved the music, and he gave the music freely and prodigiously in every direction—360 degrees he gave of himself. It wasn't about contest and competition and taking first, second, or third prize. It was not like that for him. It was about having his voice and sharing the music outside himself. He was a master who knew how to give. It was not a zero-sum game. When you give something to other people, you do not lose from that. It is not a competition. Stub lived that.

Alma Carrington, MD

I first met John as a patient when he was assigned to my services in Calvary Hospital in the Bronx, NY, in 2005. My first impression was that he was a very determined man. He knew his illness and he was determined to survive despite all odds. In his initial evaluation, he told me about his love for music and that he was an accomplished musician. He absolutely loved music. He told me he knew he was sick, but he would do all he could to fight the disease. I had a lot of respect for his will to fight the illness.

I listened to his music on the internet. My father was a musician, and for me jazz was a part of my life. Before some of the popular music, I knew Miles Davis, Quincy Jones, Nancy Wilson—this is what I grew up with. I knew about the jazz music in Harlem. I heard Count Basie, and I would sit there through the rehearsals. John and I would often talk about all the places we knew together, and he realized I understood what it was like to be a musician. I had a great respect for musicians, especially jazz musicians. My father played the piano. I was very familiar with the music, the sets, gigs, and Ella Fitzgerald.

When former President Bill Clinton visited him at Calvary, it was a big thing. Before he came, John told me President Clinton played the sax and he knew him in Arkansas. It was an amazing day to have this type of person come to visit a patient—a patient who was my patient. President Clinton was so unassuming. He made the Secret Service crazy because he wanted to stop and talk to patients, which was simply his character.

For the staff, it was an experience of a lifetime. We had Bill Clinton coming into Calvary Hospital, and we wanted everything on the floor tiptop. The hospital was immaculate. It was glistening. The director of medicine was throwing things behind the door to make sure nothing was in the way. The stairwells were all closed off. Everything was on the down-low for security. The CEO of the hospital was notified he was coming, and the Secret Service called on the way and gave a blow-by-blow of their arrival. They had extra security officers called in to make sure everything was done the right way. When President Clinton came into John's room, he stayed a long time. After he finished with John, he went down the hall visiting with patients. Families were so glad he was there. He was in no rush to leave.

John was so funny. I remember once he told me confidentially, "You know, sister Joyce—she is in charge. She is so much smarter than I am. She knows what's happening at all times with me. When I am not able to know, I want to make sure that Joyce knows." That was the respect he had for her.

John was an accomplished musician. He loved life. He loved people. He liked to talk very much, and he loved the music. Certain people are born to be what they are and what they do. John was born to be a musician. That was his life, and he lived it to the fullest until God called him home. He transitioned peacefully and with dignity and compassion, which he absolutely deserved.

Andy Collins

I first met John shortly after the album "Quickstep" was released in about 1992. Kenny Barron was the leader of this date, and his band mates were John on tenor sax, Eddie "Doc" Henderson on trumpet, David Williams on bass, and Victor Lewis on drums.

My long-time friend, the late Jimmy Heath, introduced us in Queens, NY. I learned that John was from Little Rock, which became my home in 1986. On my next trip to New York, where I lived and worked while I was a tax attorney (and still have many friends and business associates), I took John to dinner, and we got to know each other. It was a nice restaurant, and I insisted that I was buying dinner. After dinner, we went to hear jazz at a club where John was well known. We each had a few drinks, and when I asked for a check, I was told "on the house." John was warm, funny, and grounded, and we had a quick rapport. He knew I understood his world (Jazz) and I admired that he left Little Rock to be a jazz musician. I respected that he always seemed to be "gigging."

Between 1992 and 1996, I was in New York for various reasons and tried to see my new friend John while I was there. Many times, he was traveling or busy working, but we hung out plenty. We shared stories that proved that all "jazz giants" were human, and John was a good storyteller.

Sometime in 1995, I invited John to perform at my Wildwood Jazz Festival in June of 1996. He couldn't commit because he was so busy but in early 1996, he told me that the same band that recorded "Quickstep" would love to perform. The only person I had not contracted with by March of 1996 was my former West Coast friend/neighbor, Joe Henderson. His manager was difficult and would not let me speak directly with Joe, but I liked him so much that I overpaid and agreed to fly him and the other New York acts down, thanks to a generous friend offering his private jets.

John loved how McCoy Tyner thought and played as a jazz musician, as did I. One day in New York, John and I were talking music theory, and he spent a full hour explaining how McCoy used the pentatonic scale when he played the blues. We were at a piano and as Bubba (John's nickname) explained McCoy's use of the minor pentatonic scale over dominant chords, I played what he described, and he would say, like a child, "That's it!" or "No, let me show you."

My memories of Bubba are mundane because we usually laughed the hardest when we were just sharing a meal or hanging out. John enjoyed my impersonations of jazz musicians we both knew, and I loved his stories of jazz life.

It was only during the time he was in Little Rock that John talked with me about his idol, his sister Joyce. He called Joyce "the finest person I know," and I finally got to meet her over dinner in Little Rock with John, the great Sam Rivers, and Sam's young bassist and drummer. John's admiration of Joyce was evident. Knowing Joyce now, I completely understand John's feelings.

John was attractive, dressed well, and was, candidly, a magnet for attractive women. Whether he knew these women or not, he was always polite and respectful. He never discussed his love life with me, but it was pretty obvious that he had a robust one.

Looking at all the disparate jazz musicians John played with—from Miles to Anthony Braxton to Stan Cowell to McCoy to the avant-garde "royalty" such as Lester Bowie, Julius Hemphill, and Joseph Jarman—one gets a better sense of Bubba's musical range and vocabulary. As Jimmy Heath said, "He is a polyglot."

I hope John Stubblefield is remembered for his exceptional body of work as a jazz musician as well as a great, stand-up human being. He was well-mannered, rarely lost his cool, and was respected by his fellow musicians. He was one of the really fine people in the jazz world and played the soprano saxophone as well as any sax player I am aware of.

Jimmy Davis

John and I grew up in the same neighborhood in the South End of Little Rock. I called him "Stub." I lived at 2929 Chester and John at 3105 Chester. Where we grew up is like a ghost town now, but when we were there, the neighborhood was alive and kids were everywhere. We attended the same schools, Booker T. Washington Elementary, Dunbar Junior High School, and Horace Mann High School. As boys, we hung out together in the neighborhood, played marbles, rode bikes, and spent time at the local neighborhood grocery store, Morgan's.

Stub was an outstanding musician. He was extraordinaire as a saxophonist and flautist. His improvisation was exemplary. I will never forget the time I was present and heard him play with Nat Adderley. It was phenomenal. John played his butt off. I went to many of his concerts and while there, I experienced his expertise in circular breathing. What I liked about his use of this difficult technique was how he mastered it in his delivery and could hold a note forever. Stub was a player who really handled his craft. Stub, Louis Smith (another classmate), and I all played in the band from junior high school through college. Stub and Louis would sneak out and go down on Nineth Street to the clubs and play as teenagers. I did not go. I would tell them, "You guys have a mom and dad. I do not." You see, my dad passed away when I was 11 years old.

Stub developed a craft, an ability to create his sound. When he would be playing, there were certain techniques he would apply to make the sound his own. As I said, he could hold a note for an extraordinary length of time using the circular breathing technique. I have observed Stub holding a note for four or five minutes if he so desired. He played from his soul.

I remember when we entered Dunbar Junior High School, Mrs. Clay was our band director. This was the early stages of our musical instructions. When we graduated to Horace Mann High School, we had the opportunity to play a lot for school programs, socials, and assemblies. John played at just about every program. When we finished high school, both John and I entered AM&N College in Pine Bluff, Arkansas. At AM&N College, we were expected to have knowledge of all instruments in the event we became band directors; consequently, we were encouraged to learn to play as many instruments as possible.

John took advantage of this by playing saxophones, flutes, clarinet, oboe, French horn, etc. Our band director was Harold Strong. I recall we had a nickname for him—"Juice." Stub was in the concert, marching, and jazz bands. The band director was very intense and would make us practice for hours. We developed a chant we would all sing together when we had had enough. "Juice, Juice, Turn Me Loose." We would sing that loud, and sometimes he would lighten up and others he would not. Harold Strong had a purpose for each of us. That goal was to study and be committed to the music. There was a lot of discipline, and we played the music repetitively with a purpose. We paid our dues, finished school, stayed out of the war, and went into the world. I became an educator and Stub a jazz musician.

In one of our conversations, we discussed how he felt about his music. He expressed to me that he loved what he did, that music was like a religion to him. He then told me he had a series of prayers he would pray at certain times and on certain days regarding his music. This was obviously the spiritual side of him with this commitment to daily prayer.

One concern Stub discussed with me on more than one occasion was that early in his career some musicians appeared to question his ability to take the spot of Cannonball Adderley when Cannonball transitioned. He felt he was prepared to grow in that position, and as far as I am concerned, I felt sure Stub was more than prepared to replace anyone. He was a superior musician who played many instruments.

I was visiting in Little Rock not long ago and picked up an article about Stub. In that article, they gave glorified remarks about Stub. It went on to say he had done extremely well and his biggest accomplishments were outside the state of Arkansas. I am proud of Stub, my neighbor, my friend.

The last time I heard Stub play, he did a concert in Milwaukee and I was there. Stub was the featured player, and what a magical jazz sound he produced that night. I will never forget that night.

Stub was true. Stub had the ability to draw people into his music. It was "like magic." He was a superior musician. He was outstanding on any instrument he picked up. When Stub played, it was "like magic." When he touched it, it was "like magic." It takes a special person to develop a magical sound, and Stub did just that. This is one fact I do not want anyone to forget. He just played, and I repeat—that factor within him was "like magic."

Wayne Escoffery

The very first time I met John was when I went to West End. I was in high school and went to hear his band play. I had heard a lot about him. I knew he had played with Kenny Barron. I recall this performance at the Westend was very powerful.

Musically, I considered John to be a jazz master. While in high school, I spent a lot of time listening to the masters—Art Blakley, Woody Shaw, Charley Mingus. John and Eddie Henderson studied, played, and spent a lot of time with those masters. They were my guiding light. I wanted to model myself after them as a strong, dignified musician. When I finally got to know John, it made me feel great that he was welcoming and encouraging. You know some musicians are just not like that. John was among the masters, and I looked up to him and wanted to emulate him.

John was such a well-rounded musician and educator. Seldom do you find a multi-woodwind instrumentalist. John was a multi-woodwind instrumentalist and the full picture of a very well-rounded musician.

I was a fan of Dexter Gordon and knew how important he was as a tenor sax player. There are other sax players when you hear them play, you do not hear the Dexter Gordon influence in their playing. I had heard John on a Kenny Barron recording and had not realized how much Dexter Gordon influence was in his playing. It really moved me that John was influenced by Dexter Gordon and it was a joy to hear him perform.

When I joined the Mingus Band, though, I heard the Dexter Gordon influence from John, but in addition to that I heard so many other influences at once—like George Adams, John Coltrane, and a variety of other influential players. John was open minded, and he had not just one influence but many in his music.

Once when we were on the road taking a long bus ride, John played a tape and asked me to listen and let him know who I thought was playing. To me it sounded like Miles Davis back in the '60s. I then asked John if it was Wayne Shorter. He said, "No, man, This is me with my band." Here I saw another transformation in John's music with influence from Wayne Shorter. I was surprised I did not recognize it was John playing and not Wayne. John now had the Wayne Shorter influence! John really embraced a lot of facets of music, and that memory will always be with me.

John was the "real deal." He exemplified what a great musician should be. Well-schooled, full of soul, and very open minded musically. Again, John was both welcoming and encouraging. He was a selfless person musically and personally. Sometimes in this business, you get caught up in self, but John was not like that. He shared his knowledge with other musicians freely. He thought of others. For humanity to survive, we must remember that we must nurture and mentor others and be open minded as John was to me and as Mingus and others were to John. We would all be in a better place if many would grasp this concept.

Douglas Ewart

I met John in 1968 at the time the Association for the Advancement of Creative Musicians (AACM) was at the Parkway Community Center in Chicago, Illinois. I am not sure how Stub got introduced to the AACM, but I would frequently see him at AACM gatherings. He later began playing with different ensembles, smaller groups, and with Muhal Richard Abrams' ensemble, one of the original founders of the AACM. The AACM was a good organization that attracted many talented musicians. It was different in that it attracted the exploratory and younger musicians. John came along early in the development of the organization. As the AACM grew, musicians began to transition from Chicago to New York and Europe. John chose New York.

When I met Stub, I thought he was older than me and had been playing for a while. I later found out he was just a year older than me. Stub was easy to get along with. He was one of those people you meet and you just mesh. We called him Stubblefield at first more than John, then finally he was Stub. He was very friendly and encouraging. When we met, the AACM was running a training program, and Muhal Richard Abrams was our instructor. He was a highly experienced musician having played with many of the masters. Muhal was a prolific composer and theorist who studied and taught Joseph Schillinger's work. Stub and I were a part of these classes, which were based on mathematics. Muhal was really into it, and we learned that theory and used it in the development of our own voice.

John was a consummate arranger, composer, and educator. He had that dynamic personality, and we got along really well together. Stub was tremendous early on. I got to see him grow as a musician. While in Chicago, Stub was impacted by the master artists he met and played with (e.g., Lester Bowie, Leroy Jenkins, Joseph Jarmon, Claudine Myers, etc.). Ironically, several of the members of the AACM were from Arkansas since this was during the time of the migration of Black people from the South to the North. After all, there were more opportunities and possibilities for work in Chicago. Chicago was more open than the southern areas from where they migrated. Stub, along with Maurice McIntyre, John Jackson, Joseph Jarmon, Claudine Myers, and others from Arkansas took advantage of the pivotal opportunity to move to Chicago to embrace and experience the possibilities for Black people there. Musically, Chicago was very advanced, and that is where Stub landed, being taught by and playing with many of the masters in music at that time. So as a musician, he established his professional foundation in Arkansas, Chicago, and then on to New York, where he always said, "New York is where the Music is."

Stub was a great tenor saxophone player. Additionally, he played alto, soprano, clarinet, flute, and piano—but his primary instrument was the tenor saxophone. Stub was quite a writer and orchestrator. Like many musicians, he was well educated. He taught in the Chicago Public Schools and later served as professor of music at Rutgers University, so while continuing to travel and play the music, he also was sharing the music from the prospective of an educator. As a musician, Stub was a part of the holistic movement, a lively group, not only in music but in visual arts, dance, etc. When Stub came to Chicago, things were in high gear, and the city was robust in the arts and ethnicity. He was able to develop his skills around the masters, not just masters but path finders—John Gilmore, Maurice McIntyre, Muhal Abrams, Henry Threadgill, Claudine Myers, and others. These and other experiences helped Stub develop his voice playing the tenor saxophone. It allowed him to become his own visionary as a saxophone player, writer, composer, and arranger.

We used to have these AACM annual meetings and there was a lot of filibustering, and I remember one time John stood up and said, "Mr. Chairman, I am going all the way out."

I used to see Stub in New York from time to time. I remember one time George Lewis and I had just returned from Europe and we ran into Stub on the street. It was routine that when musicians would meet in this way, they would be curious about what each other was doing. So, in our conversation with Stub that day, the question was "what are you pursuing?" We explained that we were just in from Italy, and we had a recording made during that time. Stub wanted to hear it. We then decided to go to George's place in the Manhattan Plaza to listen to the recording. We wanted Stub to hear it because we respected him as a musician and artist and wanted him to hear our music. While listening to the music, Stub spoke to us about our music, with specifics, enthusiasm, and encouraging thoughts.

George Lewis has written a book about the AACM entitled *A Power Stronger Than Itself*, and I recall there is a classic photograph in that book where John is holding his disassembled clarinet. It is displayed as an old time visual, and Stub is holding the clarinet deconstructed in his hand as if it were an offering. I recall this is one of the most used photographs by the AACM and Stub is in it. The photograph was taken in the backyard of Wardsworth Jarrell, a member of the group called Afro Cobra that was around during the birth of the AACM. A lot of the musicians with the AACM at that time are featured in this picture.

I recall Stub speaking highly of Gerald Wilson. Gerald led a big band in California. He had some terrific players, and Stub studied him from afar because Gerald was a noted composer and arranger and Stub wanted to know all about him. Gerald, like Stub, was a very friendly and amicable man. I believe Gerald was a distant mentor whom Stub studied and developed different techniques in his music.

I have a manuscript book that Stub wrote in while I was taking lessons from him. At that time, he was teaching me about the song "Milestones," a composition by Miles Davis. I still have that manuscript with Stub's notes. I had many great times and experiences with John.

One of the last times I saw John I was having lunch with Henry and Marsha Wilson. While eating, we stepped outside the restaurant and ran into Stub. We asked him to join us, but he said he was on his way somewhere and could not join us. I just remember whenever we saw each other there was a certain gladness we felt.

I remember that evening very well. We were so surprised to catch Stub passing by. I had many great times and experiences with John. He is greatly missed.

I would like people to remember Stub's humanity. He was a really kind soul. His nature was to be encouraging to people embarking on their music career and to share his knowledge with them. He was a great writer, composer, and arranger—and a hell of a musician. He was a great cheerleader and very encouraging to all musicians and he came out to support other musicians playing.

It was always good to see him and others from the musical family. This made us stand on our toes and be the best we could be. It gave us a different momentum to play the music and do it well. He was also strong with a fierce personality. He could be unrelenting, but very curious, probing, and as always, a consummate musician. Stub was always searching and striving to improve his work. He was a musician who found his own voice, and when we heard him play, we knew who it was, Stub. We cannot get over having lost him so early.

Joe Ford

John and I played together in the McCoy Tyner Band, Fort Apache Band (FAB), and with a musician by the name of Big Black.

John and I first met in the McCoy Tyner Big Band. We found that we had a mutual friend who was from his hometown of Little Rock. This friend was Alias Wheeler with whom I attended college at Central State. Alias actually lived on Ringo Street, which was one block west of where John grew up. I also found out that John went to school with Alias in the 70s and that Alias had a sister who John liked.

Our actual meeting was around '77 or '78, but I had known John through my affiliation with Big Black. I do not recall Big

Black's name, only that this is what everyone called him (he did percussion work). We had two rehearsals with Big Black, but things did not take off.

John and I later joined the Fort Apache Band, of which I am now the last member living. Jerry Gonzales, band leader, passed away some time ago, and his brother Andy just passed away this past week. Other members of the Fort Apache Band were Larry Willis, Carter Jefferson and John as tenor sax players, Steve Berrios, and me. John left the Fort Apache Band around the time he became ill in 2004. I recall visiting him in New York Presbyterian Hospital—that was the last time I saw him. After John left, there were many musicians bidding on taking his place, but Jerry Gonzales decided not to hire another horn player. No one wanted to have another tenor player after Carter and John.

While touring in Paris with the McCoy Tyner Big Band, John, Jr. Cook, and I went to the Vandoren music store for reeds and mouthpieces. Vandoren Paris sells high quality products and is the leader in reeds, mouthpieces, and accessories for woodwinds.

John was very acquainted with the people in the store inasmuch as he had shopped there many times. While there, John tried out a new mouthpiece that had not come to the market. He was given the mouthpiece, and the owner engraved John's name in it. John was the king of reeds; he went through reeds like candy. He was desperately searched for the perfect one. He would work on his reeds and file them down until they were perfect. He would also work on his mouthpieces until they were right too. Me, I did not fool with my reeds like that. I used what I had, licked it, and played it. I simply did not have the time or patience to work on reeds like John did. I was not in the same league as John. In addition to his working to perfect his reeds, he had a special sand paper he would work with to get his reeds right. Once he tore off a piece of the sand paper and gave it to me to use on my reeds. I think I still have that piece of sand paper. John played a lot of woodwind instruments, and with this versatility, he learned how to perfect his reeds.

The next experience I will never forget regarding John was on a tour to France with the Fort Apache Band (FAB). John had started out in the FAB before and then left. He was replaced with Carter Jefferson in the late '80s. Prior to the tour in France, Carter went to Poland on a personal tour. When he was leaving, he pledged to us that he would meet us in France at the close of his Poland tour. Unfortunately, he became ill and died in Poland. John was called back to go on the tour.

I remember John got a bottle of wine, drank it, and went to sleep under the piano in the bar where we were to play. Our manager, Todd Barken, went down and got John so he could get ready to play that night. I will never forget as we opened for the first set and I listened to John, he was not blowing as I know John blows his sax—without a doubt I knew John's sound and this was not it. As he blew, we began to stare at him. He was *blowing just like Carter*. His sound and everything was that of Carter. It was strange to say the least. After that set, we were all amazed. When we began the second set, John played like JOHN. We were all convinced that Carter honored his commitment. He did meet us in France that night—by playing through John. It was scary, but Carter had told us he was going to meet us in France and he did. In the second set, John returned and played the style that we all knew to be his.

On another occasion, I remember we were on tour and John had purchased a new horn case for his tenor. It was heavy, so I asked him why he bought it since it was heavy and gave him fits with his back. I told him the case was too heavy to carry around in the airport. He needed a lighter case. I added, the case was breaking him down and I would throw that thing in the ocean. While walking in the airport, I looked around and John had disappeared. When I saw him again, he had purchased a luggage carrier for his case. He had that big "John" smile on his face. We arrived home, and John replaced the case.

Finally, on a personal note, this experience involved me and my family. We were playing with the McCoy Tyner Big Band in a club in NYC. On occasion, I would bring my family to hear the band play. On this night, Sunday, I brought my wife, son, and daughter with me. The children were young, perhaps between the ages of six or seven. Of course children are restless at that age and sometimes need something else to focus on. To keep my daughter quiet, my wife took her bracelet off and gave it to her. When the set was over, my daughter had dropped the bracelet and we could not find it anywhere. John found the bracelet that night after we left. He called to let me know he had found the bracelet where we were sitting and that he would place it in the mail. I always thought that was the nicest thing. He was a nice and thoughtful brother. It was always good to talk to him. You could not be mad with John.

What I would like people to remember about John Stubblefield is that he was a great guy, nice man, thoughtful for others, and music gave him new life.

Alex Foster

I am not sure if John and I first met in California or New York City, but I recall our first meeting in New York back in the 70s. It was in the Soho area, which was where artists gathered to jam and socialize. It was a 24-hour thing just hanging out. Back then, this was an area with a lot of uninhabited lofts, and people just moved in as squatters. Things had not been developed in the area. There were empty factories that had been left behind. The lofts were very spacious (2,000 to 3,000 square feet), and the artists just moved in. The area was great because it was an underground art scene with music and art, and everyone enjoyed that scene. I enjoyed being there because of the music. This is when I first met John in the city.

My first impression of John was he was friendly, very approachable, and comfortable with people. He was a people person. He was consistent through the 45 years I knew him. He was always the same guy. Same kind of dedication to the music. He was interested in exchanging information with people. He was very much alive. It all came from his spirit, confidence, and his mission in life. You never had to wonder what he was thinking because he would tell you. I watched him. He was inspirational and sensitive. He pushed the younger musicians to get involved. He gave the Mingus Band a personality that did not exist in big band music beforehand.

John was about engaging with the audience. He had a way of reaching out to them. He gave 100% when he was performing, especially when he stood up to play his solos. He had a clear vision of what he wanted people to understand about the journey of the music. He knew the energy he wanted to move in the room, and that energy explained what he was saying musically.

John was an iconic musician. I miss his energy, fashion, and dedication. His sense of caring was contagious. The intensity of what he did on the bandstand projected itself to the emotions of the audience. He liked to go over the top when he performed. One of his sayings was "We got red meat out there." Certainly, John is missed by members of the Mingus Band. He was the heartbeat of the band.

The kind of character John possessed is no longer active as I see it. The one thing that surprised me is when he was ill, he sat in his bed and wrote music. I found out how detailed his writing was for the band. Suddenly, he had written about three or four arrangements for the Mingus Big Band while he was ill. We recorded many times before John got sick, and I never saw him write charts for the band. I think he said to himself, "There is something I have to leave with the band. I have a little more to say," and he wrote these wonderful charts that we still play. I can imagine him thinking, "I am going to give it to you like this."

John loved Mingus, and he felt a passion and a need to leave this behind for us. This completely surprised me. I recall playing with him in McCoy Tyner's band. To my knowledge, he never brought charts there either. John inherited George Adams's seat as tenor in the Mingus Band, and he knew he was sitting in a chair that he knew he had to bring it. John met and exceeded that challenge, and we are fortunate that this lineage has been passed on and remains powerful.

I recall once our road manager, Albert Sun, was giving some instructions while we were on the road. While Albert was giving information, John casually said to him, "We got the music, Mr. Sun—this is how we are going to go down."

I recall once John got mad with me because I called something on the fly. He got such an attitude with me regarding who would play the second solo. He felt without a doubt if there were two tenor solos, he had to have one of them. I came to understand that he felt he was there and he was there to be heard, and I had crossed the line on that. John had to have one of those solos, and that was not optional. I could tell by his reactions and he was clear on how he felt, and I understood why.

The last trip I was on with John, I knew something was not right. At several times I heard him make the saying, "Yes, Lord, I know." It was clear he was having problems walking to the gate. Once the decline started, it was fast. I visited him in the hospital, and he looked good. I used to go with Sue Mingus and Frank Kuumba Lacy to the hospital to visit him. He was strong.

John was a major force on the American music scene as a player, arranger, composer, and a friend to a lot of musicians. John is missed. I think about him all the time. He is still with us. I have my memories and those powerful recordings he has produced. We were all touched by John. He had an iconic personality we will never forget. I will always have fond memories of him.

Olivier Gatto

My first encounter with John was by listening to his music on the *Confessin'* album back in 1985. A friend of mine in Bordeaux gave me that LP and told me, "I am sure you're going to dig that recording." I was listening to jazz music as far back as I can remember (four years old), and I was known, still now, to be very picky. I immediately liked his playing, his writing, and his passionate style. I could connect to it in many levels: tradition, swing, intensity, blues, storytelling. Then I bought *Bushman Song* and Kenny Barron's Quintet iconic *What If?*, and I was hooked.

In 1988 John came to Boston, I think with the Henry Threadgill group. I was studying at Berklee College at that time, and I went to the concert and introduced myself to John. I told him I liked a lot his music and that I transcribed his tenor solo on "Voyage." I asked him when and where he would be playing next, and he told me he would be performing in Paris soon with Kenny's Quintet. He gave me his card and told me to stay in touch. Finally, when he came to Paris, he very kindly put me on the guest list. After the show, we talked and we hung for a while. This is how our friendship started.

I left Boston in 1989, started to tour in Europe. I played with John for the first time early 1990. We talked for endless hours. We also crossed paths on the road. I remember one epic jam session that happened in Bordeaux while I was playing with Joe Henderson and George Cables. McCoy Tyner, Junior Cook, Frank Lacy, and John came to sit in.

John met my parents. He and my dad hooked up easily around their common love: the saxophone and cigarettes. I moved to

Greece fall 1991 and brought John a few times there to play. We even did an unissued recording, *Here and There* with Billy Cobham and George Cables. We recorded three compositions of John's, among them the title track.

John graciously brought me a few times to the States to perform with his Quartet or his group "Quiet Fire." I still have the bass book for that band. Early 2000, John went full-time with the Mingus Big Band, and our collaboration on stage was less active. We were both very busy. At that time I was living in Paris, but we remained in contact as usual with endless phone calls, talks on music, with postcards and mails that John always sent me including his compositions, arrangements, and parts, books that I should read, and music books that I should be aware of.

The last time I saw John was in July 2002 when my first child was born. He played close to Bordeaux with the Mingus BB, and as usual we hung out, and he played with my three-month-old boy and we took pictures.

On April 10, 2004, after five days at the hospital, my dad passed away. Such a sudden death (we thought he had just a flu) left me a bit disoriented, but I remember calling my closest friends, telling them the news, and getting their support. Strangely I didn't hear from John. I remember being in Provence and speaking on the phone with Kenny Rampton who told me that John was at the hospital very sick, and he gave me the room phone number.

I called John, spoke with Katherine who told me that he wasn't able to speak to me and that I shouldn't tell him about my dad. I called a few other times, and I was never able to speak to John. Basically, it was never the right moment. Time passed. I had to help my mom who was going through a hard phase. She was recovering from cancer and she had lost the love of her life. Later that year I spoke with Kenny Rampton and said I wanted to come to NYC and was planning to visit John in spring 2005. Kenny told me that maybe I should not come, but that John was always speaking about me. I finally didn't come, tried to call John, but couldn't get through. Time flew, and early July 2005, I saw the Mingus Big Band in Bordeaux. That afternoon at the soundcheck, they told me that John passed away. I always regret that I didn't push more to get him on the phone and that I didn't go to NY to see him.

John and I talked a lot! I remember my phone bills coming in from talking to him back in the days when one minute overseas was one dollar. He was more than a good friend. He was my mentor, along with Joe Henderson, and also part of our family, always sending presents to my niece, nephews. I miss those long conversations. I miss looking at the Superbowl with him. I miss asking him for advice. I miss him passing on parts of the oral tradition of the Black American Music.

After John's transition, it took me more than 10 years to listen to his music. Finally, I told myself, "Okay, you are 57 years old. He would be 75 this year. We had our small games about numerology. It is time to move forward, open his music collection, and start to play it again.

I have mostly all of John's music, a full portfolio. When his brother, William Stubblefield, transitioned in 2001, John wrote an elegy to him. I have a copy of that music. It was a powerful piece that helped John establish some closure for this death. He wrote a song for me "Olivier's Delight"—funny because he wrote it with a "Latin Jazz" flavor as he predicted I was going to marry a Puerto-Rican lady who's also a great flutist and saxophonist. We spoke a lot about Mary Lou Williams. He told me she taught him how to write music, how to link his music in the tradition while expending it, and among many counsels that every composition needs at least a break. Every time I play John's music when I reach the break, I think about Mary Lou, and of course all my compositions have a break.

Playing with John was amazing. Like going to church, many times the Holy Spirit was coming down, and we were going to a different place that most of our generation weren't used to. The first time I played with him, he started to count the tempo, then bang the ground with his foot, and the whole rhythm section felt lifted up. The level of intensity never dropped, and the energy he gave was something I never experienced. John played and lived every note. John wasn't a musician—he was Music. By Music, I don't mean a more or less sophisticated sounds organization. I mean the moment when the only thing you can say when you finish playing is "That's it!" Nothing less. Nothing more. In an artist's career few are the moments like that, and fewer are the artists able to bring that on stage. John was one of them.

We once took a three-hour train ride from Bordeaux to Paris, then a plane to Greece. I've reflected on our personalities during that trip. I thought of how John and I got along even though I did not drink, smoke, or do any drugs, and he was quite the opposite. I really wonder how we got along, but I remember he was joking a lot during that tour especially when we were playing George's composition "Dark Side, Light Side" and also telling me that when we met I looked like Jesus. He started to freak out because everywhere he was going to play, I was always coming out of nowhere surrounded by light as an apparition. In spite of our differences, we always respected each other, and we got along very well together. We were part of the Aquarian Brotherhood as he was always saying.

On the other hand, John was very funny and had a strong and real sense of humor, full of exaggerations very similar to the Mediterranean spirit that one can find in Marseilles or Naples. That is probably why he also felt at home with my parents. We had one silly tradition together: every time we met, first thing was to go to a fast food place and order a couple of burgers. John was always eating the meat but not the bread. Once I said, "Why do you leave the bread?" and he said, "Because the bread makes you fat."

John brought me everywhere he could, introduced me to countless musicians, artists, we shared birthday parties, and I had his back a few times. But he was a very private person too. For example, I never had the opportunity to visit his apartment, but he apologized about that once and invited me to dinner to his girlfriend's place. This is how I met Marsha Heydt. Then we went to see the great Billy Harper playing with his quintet. It was a great experience to have two charismatic artists in the same room.

Currently, I am taking care of my family: three boys and a beautiful wife. We also have my mom next door, and we help her too as she helps us. We perpetuate the Latin tradition to have Grand Ma at home. Family is important. A transgenerational home is crucial for the balance of all and the passing of wiseness.

As the world is engaged with the Coronavirus pandemic, we are in France coming out slowly of the confinement, and for artists the future is questionable. For the first time in 34 years, I have no idea if I will be playing music next year professionally, if I can plan anything, but I do remember "Therefore do not worry about tomorrow, for tomorrow will worry about itself. Each day has enough trouble of its own." So I go back to study music, open the books John gave me, new books, PhD thesis, anything that will help me to complete what John always called "Olivier's Vision," and I hear his voice while introducing me to the audience, "Olivier Gatto on bass, the man with a plan, a man of vision."

What I want people to remember about John is that he was one of the greatest musicians of the 20th century. He was ahead of his time in many ways, a precursor. He would have fit perfectly in the music scene of today where all Black American Musical Tradition is combined in a vivid artistic way. He was also a great composer, and we worked a lot together on a project of publishing his work. He was always focused on writing singable melodies. Even his more complex compositions have a great melody. Many critics and musicians put John as a follower of

Wayne Shorter, ignoring John's compositions and exploration of the blues, but while I played with him, I heard all the history of saxophone in the jazz mold in a very strong and unique presentation, not at all an artificial patchwork. I could hear Lester, Hawk, Hodges, Don Byas, Bird, Trane, Wayne, Ayler. Of course his being married to an American woman for nine years who was the daughter of a pastor, a whole aspect of John's musical personality, the hidden part of the iceberg for me, appeared—the highly spiritual essence of his music.

I have been blessed to have known John, to have performed with him and lived something rare in performing arts: Entering the Zone.

A life-changing experience. Unfortunately, recordings can represent just a little bit of what John was: a complex, fascinating, charming, generous human being who openly welcomed and helped anybody who was sincere in his love to learn about Afro-American Music. Overall he was one of the greatest American contributors to 20th Century World Music.

Dick Griffin

I met John in Chicago while playing with Roland Kirk. I recall it was during a matinee in a jazz club there. We played in the basement. During that time, every saxophone player that was not working would come out to hear Roland Kirk. Sonny Rollins and all the baddest players would come out to hear him play. They would be jamming standing toe to toe and the challenge was on. Another gathering place was McKee's Fitzgerald Lounge. Here you would find saxophonists like John Griffin, Clifford Jordan, John Gilmore, R. E. Brown, and John. A lot of entertainment was there.

My first impressions of John were his smile and generosity. We had a lot in common. We were both Aquarius. He was a guy who had charisma. This is something that is given to you by God. You either have it or not. John had this in his playing and in his personality. It was forever present in his smile. He did have a mean streak and rightly so. Anyone living in Chicago had to develop a toughness about them. After all, it was a gangster town, and you had to learn ways to defend yourself. To survive, John developed ways to protect himself. He knew how to stand off and observe and take care of himself. In ways, I am sure this prepared him for his move to New York City in 1970. None of this took away from his ability to be there for others.

John was a dedicated and talented musician. He lived the music! He was a great musician who knew a lot about music, writing, arranging, and playing. He read a lot and was very prolific in his writing. He always came up to the challenge. He played with a lot of big bands during his career.

When John moved to New York in 1970, we lived in the same neighborhood. He was married to Sharon, and their son, John, was born in 1973. During that time, I was really busy playing, teaching, and doing house bands in Harlem. John and I would go over to Miles Davis's house and just hang out. We also spent time with the Collective Black Artist group, a group formed back in the late 1960s and early 70s due to the "marginalization of musical artists and Black actors." Colby Marico was a part of the organizing of this group, and many artists spent time as a part of this group. Through the years, John and I were in different big bands, such as Frank Foster's Big Band, Gill Evans's, and later we both became members of the Mingus Big Band.

I recall Mingus received a Guggenheim grant in the 1970s and formed the Mingus Big Band. He used two trombones, two trumpets, tuba, French horn, saxophones (baritone, alto), piano, and drummer. We stayed together for two years. John and I were original members of that band. Although Mingus was hard to get along with at times, I loved the way each composition he wrote had meaning.

It is noted that John and Mingus had a falling out and John left the band. This was not just a chance happening for John. Many of the band members were in and out. I remember one night we were playing at the Village Vanguard, and Mingus started to change notes on me several times. I followed his lead as best I could and when the gig was over, I went home wondering why he had done that. These changes were not only obvious to me, but also to the other players. Later that night my phone rang and it was Mingus. He said to me, "I owe you an apology, and do you need a draw." I could not believe he was calling me, but I knew this was an indication that he trusted me.

He then told me he was mad at me because previously I could not make practice and I'd sent a replacement and on one occasion I was late. I had no idea he had held that against me. He went on to tell me if I was going to send a substitute, that person had to play as good as me. He further stated I was the only person that impressed him—when he changed those keys on me, I was able to follow him. From then on, I could do no wrong.

As with John, who played with Mingus a lot, he came to know and understand the music as Mingus saw it, and this carried on until his transition. You could easily say or do something to get on Mingus's bad side, but he and John bonded musically.

I remember John writing music that had a commercial appeal, which was not keen with the AACM; however, John incorporated the past, present, and future into his music. He played experimental music.

John and I would talk on the phone for hours (six or seven). He had a clever way of drawing me into his long stories and hooking me in to hear the end. Also, when I had a real challenge in my life, I only needed to give John a call, and he would be there. He always stuck by my side.

John was a very, very kind individual that you do not find these days. He had a big heart; he was a giver and a dedicated and excellent musician. He was a dad who loved his son. He was kind and had a warm heart and was a dedicated good friend that anyone would love to have had. He was my friend.

Cleave Guyton

I used to see John a lot in the city in spots where musicians hung out, such as Bradley's, the Village Gate, Blue Note, etc. He was a really working cat. He was always busy playing with a lot of different bands. A lot of people wanted John in their bands. I saw him a lot while hanging out in different places and on the road.

He was a great musician, nice guy, friendly. He had a beautiful sound on the tenor saxophone. He was a well-polished machine. He was very knowledgeable about music. The proof was in the pudding; this is why he worked so much. Bands knew he was a great musician, and they wanted him to play in their band.

One time I will never forget was when we were playing the New Orleans Jazz Festival and I was hanging out with Earl Turpentine, John Hicks, and John at the bar in the hotel. I ended up overstaying my time with them and missed my flight home.

While John and I did not play in the same bands, we were busy on the circuit playing internationally. We played different jazz festivals all over the world. We would see each other in many different places. It was interesting. In later years as musicians, many times we did not see each other in the city, but when on the road, we were able to see each other and catch up while having a great time playing the festivals.

John was a great musician and an all-around nice guy. That is why he worked all the time and was sought out by so many bands. John had an incredible life traveling all over the world with the greatest bands in the world. You cannot ask for more. John had a ball. "You can't get better than that."

Gary Hammon

The first time I saw John was on TV playing with Billy Harper. At that time when I saw him, there was no doubt in my mind what I wanted to do.

I later met John through my friend and brother John Bush. John Stubblefield and John Bush attended school together in Little Rock. John S. had heard about me through John B. prior to our first meeting. John B. contacted me regarding John S. coming to Boston to play. I went to the concert where he was performing with Mtume, Jimmy Heath, and Cecil and Dee Dee Bridgewater. After the concert, he and I met for the first time. John and I came to my home and stayed. I recall dismantling my bed and giving him the mattress and me the box springs. We listened to music and talked until we fell asleep. We talked about any and everything pertaining to music and things going on in New York. Our relationship grew from there. The first meeting was amazing in that John B. made sure John S. and I got to know each other. After that meeting, John S. and I were in contact often.

He and I did a lot of jam sessions together, and we played together in South Africa. John was with the Masters. Stories have to be told to put things in order. A new generation of musicians was brought in and somehow ruled out John's generation. The younger generation was ushered in so quickly, and those who studied with the Masters were quickly forgotten. Little did they know that rap music was developed from the music of the past. John and I understood, and we valued what went on before. It was a struggle, but we recognized the gaps and struggled not to lose what the Masters had created. This gap between the Masters and the younger generation—like John and the new music ideology— has to be closed. The Masters individualized their music—there was no assembly line effect where everyone sounded alike.

John was a great musician. Articles talk of his talent and the recognition he did not receive. The fact of the matter is John did not go far because he did not choose to play "cookie cutter" music. John did not give in to repetitive cords—*his music was from the heart and soul with great improvisation.* Any other music John saw as illegitimate.

Not only was John a hell of a musician, he was also a beautiful person. I believe John saw in me how he was as he was developing and studying his craft. John came along when the elders wanted to know if you were serious about the music. You had to earn it. This helped develop John. He was an inspiration, and I really loved him as a musician and friend. He spent time with me because he really saw something in me. He taught me that I had to work for it. It never ends—I am still working.

I remember when I was working at this club called "Wally's" (one of the first African Americans to own a club and have a liquor license in New England). John went with me to my gig, and he sat there and listened. He was tired because he had been on the road other places and chose not to play that night. I took him around the city and we had a really good time. John called John Bush and told him he was impressed with me. John S. told me, "You know what you need to do? You just need to leave Boston and go to New York." Coming from John that was big for me. At that time, I was young and I did not have the confidence I needed. I did not feel I was ready to make that move—eventually I did make the move.

I recall a gig where John, Sonelius Smith, Benny Wallace, J.R. Mitchell, and I were playing. John played a ballad called "Sabrina." It was beautiful. It was nice because John really played that tune very well, and most of all I was there playing with him. Another memorable time was when my girlfriend and I invited John to dinner. We all had a great time together, just hanging out. It was a surprise just to have John there with us.

My biggest memory is when I met John at the Vanguard to see Joe Henderson. When I came in, John got ready to introduce me to Joe, and Joe told John he already knew me.

I remember how John would share information with me about reeds, arranging music and many other things related to music. He was very knowledgeable and wrote beautiful tunes. I will always remember him as inspiring and encouraging.

Last, but most important, John helped a lot of young musicians get started in their careers. One specifically I recall was Vincent Herring who is now a major alto player. He and many other musicians took lessons from John privately, and of course John shared his knowledge at Jazzmobile for years with many students. Again, John helped a lot of musicians become who they are today. I find it interesting that John often told me about people who encouraged him, but those who he helped seldom acknowledged the training they received from him.

John studied with the Masters. I want people to remember John by listening to his music and getting to know John the artist. Know the culture and learn about John Stubblefield. His work is documented, and you can buy his music. He played with many bands and had his own band, "Quiet Fire." He traveled the world and is better known in Europe than the United States. He was a major in his field. Generations to come need to know about him. John was a highly respected musician, and I was lucky to play with him. I loved and respected him.

Craig Handy

Wow! John's personality was so big. My very first impression was "this is a true world-class gentleman," because he was so well spoken and well mannered. He just impressed the heck out of me with his ability to carry himself with such an air of dignity and grace. His use of the English language! He sent me to the dictionary all the time.

Musically, what John became was the heart and soul of the Mingus Band. At the end of the night, John would come back with the most profound solos that made us realize there was nothing more profound than knowing how to communicate on your instrument. Mingus wrote a lot of different kinds of music, and John was aware of this. The culture was from the blues, early rock and roll, and jazz. John knew this music and would let us know why we were here. He would come and say one word and bring everyone back. Everyone had admiration for John. Previous masters could play the blues and understand the blues. John was in rare company; he could play the blues that would make you want to cry or shout and holler. He would wipe the audience into a lather when he played. *That was something else.* No one could do it like John. I am glad I got to see all of that and hear him play that sound.

Playing jazz on the road can be a very tiring and stressful way to make a living, especially when you are traveling a lot. Many times, we would travel all day and not eat properly. It was not uncommon to arrive in town and have to change in 10 minutes to run to the concert. It can get very emotionally tough to do this 365 days a year. John would always fire us up. He would stand on the wings of the stage and say, "Gentlemen, there is red meat out there. Let's take it over the top." He was like the drill sergeant who got everyone ready to do battle. He would say, "Suit up or drink up and be somebody." He was full of life and energy. John was a larger-than-life personality.

I do not know where those sayings came from, but John freely gave to us with his words. He talked a lot about being in the fox hole or being the trenches. When on a tour with the band, it is like being in the trenches. It is nonstop—planes, trains, buses, three or four hours of sleep—we had to keep moving. We all understood John. On the bandstand, he equated it with being in a battle. We had to put our battle fatigues on and get ready. With this, we forged lifelong relationships with other musicians.

I recall sometimes when John would be taking a solo, he would be trying to reach a high note and it would not come up right. He would look at someone in the audience with a little frustration as if to say "I am trying to reach this note." It was like a sporting event.

I am reminded of a time I was wrapped up in my own thing. Thinking back, I see how focused and calm John was during that situation. He stood like a tall tree in the middle of the storm.

His mantra to us was to get involved! When someone was doing a solo and not really into it, he would yell out "get involved." It was the way and when he would say things that captured me. The timing was good. He was a philosopher. He could be in the moment and also see what was happening around the corner. John had more experience than we did—like a battle general. He would know how people treated the band and how things would go. He had incredible vision. He also said what needed to be said at the time it needed to be heard. Again, he had the right answer for the situation that was going on. That made me consider him the leader of men. After all, it goes back to the battlefield where he was a master tactician.

I think at the end of the day, John realized that music was a healing force. He knew that music could be used to bring people together. People should never forget he was a great musician and an amazing performer, and the emotion with which he played connected people to the music. It was like an academic exercise. He could play two notes and make people scream.

It should be remembered that John understood the power of connection and being in the moment, forgetting about all of the stuff that divides us. After all, we are all on this journey together. That was the real power of humanity, forgetting about the BS we put up with day to day. Together we can overcome anything. That is the message I got from John.

Last, we must remember that John had a gentle heart, and he understood the power of love. Everyone in a room could feel that coming from John. These are the things that come to mind when I remember John. He was one of one, a great communicator, unselfish. He knew who he was and his worth, loved people, and yes he made the world a better place. I miss him.

Philip Harper

I first met John when I was running the late night Blue Note sessions. One week John was there playing with Freddy Hubbard.

Shortly after that I met John while on the road playing with Art Blakey. John was on the road with the Fort Apache Band. We met quite often on the road playing at the same festivals.

John was definitely a big personality guy. When you met him, you didn't forget him. He was a very well rounded great musician, well versed in many styles of music and could play with anyone.

When we'd arrive on the bus at the venue, John would stand up and speak: "All right men, we have a job to do. I know that we are all men of vision, valor, and much testicular fortitude."

I would like the world to remember that John had much heart and soul.

Eddie Henderson, MD

John and I met in San Francisco. At the time I was practicing medicine. I practiced medicine in San Francisco for 12 years before moving to New York. John came to my office in the mid 70s in need of some medical papers to be signed in conjunction with an airline ticket. I knew of him, being a musician myself, and went to hear him play after than visit. John had a phenomenal memory.

After I moved from California to NYC and we began playing together, he reminded me of the first time we met in my office. He recalled that he was asked to have a seat in the waiting room, and he got mad inasmuch as he wanted to be waited on right away. Also, I drove a Ferrari at that time, and John would make sounds with his mouth emulating the sound of the car. We always got a big laugh out of how we first met.

In 1985 I moved from California to New York, and both John and I were hired by the Kenny Barron Quintet. John and I developed a close musical and personal affiliation. John was so natural and organic. While playing together, we did not have to talk. We breathed and played melodies together automatically.

I found John to be both funny and sensitive. At times, he would become moody. He would what I call "puff up" and stop speaking sporadically. When he would change in this way, it reminded me of a chameleon, changing instantly. Sometimes this behavior would go on for a week. During his last birthday party, I called him by his nickname, Bubba. He was none too happy I had learned this name and was quick to let me know he did not like my calling him by that name. He quickly got over it.

Also, we would bump heads if he felt I did not play the melody out. He would "puff up" and make me walk around the stand to return to my seat. I knew John, and this did not go on forever. I told him, "You know, John, the best way to treat you when you are in those moods is like an elephant with diarrhea." He would laugh and we would move forward. Even with these moods these things I know: we loved each other. He had a soft side—a sweetheart, great sense of humor, and he loved to laugh, and pull pranks, and was a powerful and loving man. Everyone loved John.

I remember going to Little Rock with John. I was so impressed with the hospitality and meeting his family. It was calm and embracing, and I could see the soft side of his upbringing. It was sweet, kind, gentle—not that masculine persona he sometimes chose to display. Yeah, he had a big heart and he shared his love for others both personally and through "the music."

We played music with the Mingus Band, McCoy Tyner, and Kenny Barron, to name a few. I remember recording with John on his album *Bushman Song*. He knew "the music" and played it from deep within.

What I want people to remember about John is that he was a consummate serious musician who learned and played with the "Masters." Everyone loved John; he was a prolific writer, arranger, and composer. His tone was immediately recognized. It was his signature tone. When he transitioned, he left a big gap in the music world.

I miss John; we loved each other so much.

Walter Henderson

So, my first meeting with John was in the early 60s. We were both attending Horace Mann High School in Little Rock. He was two grades ahead of me. Our meeting was centered on jamming and learning the songs and listening to the music. Later as budding musicians, five of us (John, John Bush, Robert Tresvant, James Leary, and myself) would meet at the Dunbar Community Center where we would meet and try to learn how to play and jam on tunes. We spent a lot of time doing that and just playing music. John helped raise me to play. I was just a little trumpet player in the band, and I just grew hanging with him.

My first impression of him was he was always happy. I looked to him as my big brother, my musical brother—a sibling kind of thing. We both had a passion, which was the music. As a musician, he was extraordinary because he loved to play many genres of music. He was well rounded in the different types of music. He showed me about being more diverse in selecting a myriad of things to play within the genre of jazz in particular. After he finished college, he moved to Chicago. When I graduated two years later, I also went to Chicago, again following John. We both joined the AACM.

John and I had many experiences together. Our band director in high school was Allen White, who would have us play Peter Gunn music at the football games. At times he would write and orchestrate the songs we played.

My mom had a Magnavox stereo system when John Coltrane's *A Love Supreme* album came out. John had just bought the new album, and he came to my house and we played it. We really got into the depths of the record using this stereo! My parents had jazz records and we would sit up and listen to them. During that time, being young and not having a big selection of records, anyone we were able to hear we were in seventh heaven. We listened closely to Blakely, Coltrane, Ellington, Miles, the Jazz Messengers, and others. This is how John taught, not teaching but listening to the direction of the music. We also spent many hours in the basement of John's home. We would listen to music from 10:a.m. and not finish until dark. We would just sit and listen to the music. We did not say anything to each other—just listened.

John was a light-hearted person. Both of our wives were named Sharon. I was not trying to copy him but it just happened like that. While living in Chicago, we constantly got together to listen to music, and he would come by and take me to meet other musicians. When I was with John, I was under an apprenticeship. I trailed behind him. I looked up to John quite a bit.

John taught me all about genre. Once he asked me if I knew how to play in every key (major/minor). Of course, I did not. I was more of an ear player. I now can play in any key because of John. I do not care what set I am in, I do not care what key your song is in, I can play that key. Because of John, I learned to play in every key. Again, John did not sit me down with a music lesson. We went more cosmic, more mental with things.

When I recorded my first CD John cosigned, he was a part of the liner notes. This is what he said: "I hope you like this music. I know I do."

I remember John took me to the Plugged Nickel to see Dizzy Gillespie. This was the first time I saw a vapor come out of the bell of the horn. John said, "See, he is blowing and smoke is coming out of his horn."

On another occasion, John took me to see Eddie Fisher (guitar player). I did not know who I was going to see. I was just roaming around with John. He then told me Eddie was from Little Rock, and he wanted me to come with him. I came to know Eddie Fischer through John—this great musician who made his noteworthy album *The Third Cup* and was well known in the jazz circles.

This I will never forget. My apprenticeship with John was silent, and he did not mind coming to get me to hang out with him. He spent time with me when others didn't. He was not teaching me how to play my instrument. He taught me the aesthetics of music by listening to different music directions. I will always remember how we listened to music for hours, had fun, cracked jokes, and continued our pursuit of music.

Once, John came back to Chicago with the Mingus Big Band, and he stayed with me and I got to meet the members of the Mingus Band. I took him to see some friends and relatives between sets, and we were almost late to the next gig. I was wearing a kufi hat—like an Afro Muslim type of thing. John liked the hat, and I gave it to him.

When I would visit New York, John and I would hang out and have lots of fun. He shared with me that he was one of the last tenants in his apartment where the rent had not been increased. Once while we were talking about all the people you meet as you travel through life, he spoke to the point that we were still tight after all the time that had passed. I was one of the ones who hung out with him throughout his career. His death, broke my heart.

Looking back, I can see a lot of the things that I did were influenced by John. I became a member of the AACM big band because of John. It was not long before Muhal Abrams, Henry Threadgill, and George Lewis migrated to New York just like John. I recall Michael Davis went to play with Earth Wind and Fire. I wanted to go, but by that time I had a family and stayed in Chicago.

When I was attending school at the University of Arkansas at Little Rock, I ran into the music critic Robert Palmer who was from Little Rock but lived in New York. He and John got to know each other well. Robert did a lot to help John in terms of boosting his career—he was crazy about John. Robert Palmer transitioned on November 20, 1997. In 2003 the University of Arkansas at Little Rock had its 75th anniversary celebration. Musicians paid tribute to Robert Palmer who was described as a man who cared about others. John was among those musicians who participated in that event.

I would like the world to remember that John was a great musician, and he always had a lot of people around him. He was influencing and teaching people in his way. He was personable, not a standoff person. People were drawn to him. I want people to remember his beautiful smile and that he gave mental instruction. John was a musical guru.

Note: Walter kept in touch with me during John's illness—I always knew it was Walter on the phone because of his signature voice and he would be crying. Walter transitioned on February 16, 2024. He was an excellent musician! As Walter stated in the interview, he was John's little brother, mentee, apprentice—all rolled into one. Walter Henderson will be greatly missed but never forgotten.

Conrad Herwig

I first met John when we were playing with the Henry Threadgill band, the Society Situation Orchestra. John played saxophone, and I played trombone. This must have been in the 80s. We had a lot of rehearsals and did gigs around the city. We also toured Europe with Henry's band. This is really when I got to know John. I came to the Mingus Band in 1994 or 1995, and there was John sitting right in front of me. We kept that seating arrangement for at least 15 years. Now I have been with the Mingus Band for 25 years.

John was an amazing virtuoso player. He had power and a way of building solos that drew in both the musicians and audience. I mean it drew us all in. Playing live with John, there was so much musicianship. He had such a feeling of goodwill toward musicians and others. We were really close over the years. He was always a mentor and fantastic in the band and on the road. John was the storyteller. He was the real deal, an authentic jazz musician.

He had an amazing sound. He had power, subtlety—things I observed and lessons I learned to admire and emulate. He taught me how to be compositional. It was not about playing what you know. John knew how to build on what he knew and felt as he expressed himself musically. Without a doubt he knew how to build a solo. John was the most important member of the Mingus Band. He kept us on our toes.

I recall when I took my first flight, business class, I was seated next to John. On that trip John started to mentor me. He gave me a lot of good advice. Henry Threadgill's band played from an avant-garde perspective and was in depth including be-bop and R&B. John asked me who I had played with, and he told me that he could hear the be-bop. He then said, "I will give you some advice. What you want to do is be weird, go off the charts." I tried it, and it worked out very well. John was always looking out for me and giving me advice. We became good friends in Henry's band.

I am currently the director of music at Rutgers University. John had a professorship at the university for a while. Several musicians who came to the Mingus Band were his students during his time at Rutgers. While there, John assembled a jazz ensemble and they won the Notre Dame Jazz Festival. I have the program from that festival. Again, John was such a great teacher, and he had so many lessons to teach.

I remember during one concert I was playing a solo and my slide flew all the way off into the crown at the Thyme Cafe. John simply got out of his seat picked it up and gave it back to me. I was really into that solo that night and lost my slide. This has only happened to me on two occasions. When John handed the slide back to me, he said, "A slide has no friends." As a matter of fact, I hit John a few times with my slide. He would duck out of the way. John always kept us on our toes. He had the greatest sense of humor. He was like family you know—an uncle, a brother. He was always inspiring; he had so many important things to tell.

I recall a story about John while teaching at Rutgers. John would tell his students, "I am here and you are there—you want to be here; however, they are paying me to be here. If you want to be here, you have to get your act together to be here." I have been at Rutgers for 18 years. As a musician, if you are trying to keep a playing career together, it is hard to do that and have another focus. I think some people feel their playing slips when they cannot focus fully on the playing. I think this is how John felt, and perhaps he asked himself the question, "Am I a player who teaches or a player who plays?" He was a great teacher and mentor on a day-to-day basis when he was with the band.

I remember an experience we had in Europe where one of the musicians overslept and was going to have to be left behind. John said, "No, no man left behind on our watch." We packed his suitcase and got him ready for that flight. He was not left behind. John always showed this type of kindness and love for his fellow musicians.

I was with John on his last tour in 2004. I remember we were at Ronnie Scott's, and John was ill and complained of back pain. We were concerned. He went and got acupuncture thinking it was sciatica. As his friend, I could see he was not comfortable. As I look back, I wish I would have asked him if he was getting regular checkups. At that time, he was really ill.

John was always writing, he wrote the arrangements for "The Petal Point Blues," "Orange Is the Color," "The Path of Resistance." He did not complete "The Path of Resistance." He started and transcribed the sketch for it, but it was not completed. Another musician was putting it into the computer, but I ended up finishing it. I went to visit John while he was in the hospital and we talked about that score. He told me how to finish it. He said, "It goes from a major blues to a minor blues." It was John's arrangement, but due to his illness he was not able to complete it. I finished the arrangement and I have played it a lot.

The most important things I want people to remember about John are his kindness, humanity, love of his fellow musicians as brothers and sisters. He was the most loyal and loving fellow musician of anyone I have ever known. I said to myself, that is how I want to be. I want to be like John to younger musicians. As a young musician, there was a true sense of loyalty. People handled themselves differently. This heightened sense of loyalty and awareness was evident in how musicians treated each other, how we dressed, and how we respected and trusted each other. John believed in being on time, dressing right, and playing the right thing. It was super valuable. The history of his ability to mentor will always show him as one of the all-time greats. I loved him so much. His transition was a big loss for us.

Because times have changed, it leaves me feeling my relationship with him made me a better musician, man, and dad. John was tough. He did not put up with bullshit. He was fair. He believed things should be done fair and with equity in the world. He was not cynical. I appreciated him so much. He was a loving human being and a great musician. We have to keep his legacy alive. You know the lives of musicians are tricky, complex, and we can be like a gypsy or nomad. Ideally, if John had any of these traits, I did not see it. He was an accomplished musician and a loving human being who touched the lives of others in many ways.

Sharon Seaberry Stubblefield Hunter

I met John in 1968 while completing my student teaching and completing my master's degree at Loyola University. I was a part of the Loyola Urban Studies Project where I had to student teach and set up a social services activity. I chose to set up a preschool using my students, along with their younger brothers and sisters, to complete my thesis observations. John was an itinerant music instructor in the Chicago School District. He taught classes at one of the schools where I worked, and this is how and where we met.

John and I dated from 1968 to 1971. We were married on June 21, 1971, at my mother's home in Chicago at 7034 South Perry with my sister, roommate, two brothers, stepfather, mother, and father present. Initially, John wanted me to move to New York with him before we were married; however, this did not meet my standards. This I did not want to do without a commitment. In other words, he had to "put a ring on it." And so, he did.

While we were dating, John exposed me to a lot of music! John was a member of the Association for the Advancement of Creative Musicians (AACM) and was aware of all of the jazz events in Chicago. As a member of this group, he was featured in an article in the Sunday magazine of the *Chicago Sun Times*. Because of this, my father's family accepted him more readily. We attended many jazz events together—AACM concerts, any music that came to town John wanted us to see musicians and hear the music. I recall seeing Ube Blake, Coleman Hawkins, and Duke Ellington. I recall one night being at an event where Duke Ellington was playing and there was a blizzard in Chicago. After the set, John wanted to take a picture with Duke Ellington, and Duke said, "I don't take pictures with men." While I was holding the camera prepared to take the picture, Duke said to me, "Come here, I will take a picture with a pretty girl." So, as it ended, I took the pictures with Duke.

The day John and I were married was also the last day of my master's program. John always said he wanted to be in New York City because "that is where the music is." Before the move, I was driving a Ford Torino, a graduation gift from my father. John said we needed a "flashy car," so I sold my car prior to the move. John then bought the "flashy car"—a Javelin AMC charcoal gray with red pinstripes, a true muscle car. We sold everything, emptied our bank and Chicago Public School retirement accounts, packed all we had in the car, and headed for New York in our new Javelin. I recall sleeping all the way from Chicago to New York. Upon arrival I remember John was running through red lights because they were on the side of the street rather than in the center of the street. Another thing, we could not find gas stations in this new world, the world of New York City. We stayed in a hotel until John found an apartment in a neighborhood he found acceptable, the upper east side.

John was a planner. He had researched apartments and found a nice apartment on the third floor on the upper east side—costly, yes! Our landlord was German. John wanted to contact everyone he knew in New York City when we arrived. We had no furniture; I remember the Bridgewaters gave us some chairs and a table until we could make it. We slowly bought a bed and dresser—able to get rid of the pallet on the floor and boxes for clothes. The apartment was a really nice place. We stayed there one year and then moved to a place on the west side off Broadway. I worked as a temporary secretary, and John, who was afraid to go underground and use the subways, would pick me up from work in the Javelin. I remember as we were becoming familiar with the area, we stumbled upon a dance theatre in Central Park. Dance companies from all over the world would come yearly to perform, art shows, plays etc. Although John was a musician, he was also an artist who enjoyed all forms of art. We also discovered Shakespeare in the Park and Concerts in the Park. John loved Indian food, and we frequently ate at Muharaza in the City. Next, we moved to Brooklyn across the street from the Brooklyn Academy of Music. Betty Carter, who was a jazz singer, lived on our block, Ntozake Shange, author of the Broadway play *For Colored Girls*—actually the whole block was an entertainment community. Once again, we left Brooklyn and moved to the upper west side because John needed to be "where the action was." Initially the place we found was really nice, but later the homeless people began to take over the block. We entertained a lot in our home. John liked to have people over. We remained at this location until our divorce in 1978.

Our son, John C. Stubblefield, was born in Brooklyn Jewish Hospital on February 7, 1973. I shared a room with a Hassidic female who had just had a baby, and she taught me how to breast feed. John did not accompany me to Lamaze classes; however, my friend Dee Dee Bridgewater (Glenda in *The Wiz*) did go with me. She later moved from New York City to California and then later to France. John was very slow in accepting the fact that we were pregnant. Frankly, I do not think he wanted children; however, when John was born, everything was great. I was about seven months pregnant before we told anyone about the pregnancy. At the time I was working at a daycare center, and a lady who was a midwife and one of our teachers in with the infants helped me through the pregnancy. On February 5, 1973, she told me not to come to work the next day because the baby was coming. I did not go to work. I stayed home, nesting. Later that day, I did not feel well and decided to take a bath and go to bed. In the middle of the night, I told John I thought the baby was coming and I did not feel good. He was sleepy and it was slow moving. I called a cab, and he finally got up and we went to the hospital. John's mother came and stayed with us for six weeks and was invaluable in helping me with everything. John was on a European tour during this time.

I recall Miles Davis lived near us, and John would visit with him often. He had daily jam sessions with any musicians who wanted to participate. Miles loved our baby, John C., and would not let John come in unless he had John with him. Baby John would be there with them as they jammed. John and Mary Lou Williams wrote a song about our son at the time of his birth entitled "Baby Man."

John studied different religions, Buddhist, Scientology, Moslem, etc. We attended Mosque Number 5. He bought the book *Dianetics* by L. Ron Hubbard. He chanted a mantra for hours on end at night. At one time, John became a Buddhist and tried to convince me to join, but I was not interested. There was a time around 1975 when John was turning 30 that he told me he thought he would be further along in music—that he felt that by 30 he would have accomplished his goals—but at that point he felt like a failure. Eventually, he did come through this period in his life and continued to practice and play music. This was also around the time he was called to work with Jazzmobile where he taught for many years, and he was off and running from there and continued what he loved, playing "the music."

Although we were divorced, John remained in our lives as John C. grew up. The last time I saw him was in June 2005 when we visited him in Calvary Hospital in the Bronx. He died July 4, 2005.

Ben Jones

It must have been between May 1959 and July 1960 when I think I met John Stubblefield. We were in Camden, Arkansas, at the gig where Al Hibler was the star of the show. I was already at the gig with other musicians from El Dorado when in came John and York Wilbourn and other musicians of the night.

It wasn't until five years later when I had completed four years in the military service that I met John again in Pine Bluff at AM&N College where he was already in the college band. This time I got to know John better. There he was sitting in the clarinet section with Wheatley Hill and other band members. The band at AM&N College, which we all called "The Yard," was a great band with skilled, studied musicians. They came from Chicago, Memphis, Kansas City, Arkansas, and other places. It was the band director Harold S. Strong's baton and his assistant Tyrone Tyler who instilled in us the ability to go out and make a significant place in the world as learned musicians. For example, I was a member of Tennessee and California National Guard bands. Paul Hill, a member of the trumpet section, served in the army and at Washington, D.C., among other musical positions for skilled musicians.

So, John Stubblefield was a student of music from Arkansas who emerged during a significant period for music in his home state—a time when band instrumental music was significantly a part of our community and school curriculum. He was a skilled clarinetist, flautist, oboist, composer, music instructor, and jazz soloist as he went on to distinguish himself in the field of music.

We liked John best when he took that Selmer Mark 6 out to perform. One of those musicians with extraordinary talent. He was a leader of me in music as well. He led the R&B group on campus, played gigs, and was responsible for everything involved in running a band. I was glad to see him graduate as a superior music student, move on to the Midwest as a public-school music instructor, and become a member of the world-famous Association for the Advancement of Creative Musicians (AACM).

Those who practiced music with John witnessed his ability to play "academic music" but enjoyed the ability to express his stylistic originality on the tenor sax, flute, and soprano. We loved his performance on original compositions and respected our master's performance on "Maiden Voyage" and some Miles repertoire, Art Blakey, and the music of Wayne Shorter and John Coltrane. It was in amusement and appreciation we used to sit around and observe, listen, and critique John's practice for his senior recital. This recital was required for his graduation. I noticed how diligently he practiced. He worked up a sweat!

I appreciated John's love and admiration for the musicianship of his fellow musicians—James Leary and Sonelius Smith. In addition to standard academia, these brothers were gifted and talented in jazz. I am sure their high school music teachers were great influencers, as was my teacher, Mr. Brewster.

I think the golden era of music education in Arkansas may have spanned the period 1950–1960 and perhaps beyond. That was a time when the study of the piano and wind instruments blossomed, and history will show far-back beyond those dates. But the 1950–1960 time, "that was the time" when modern jazz was greatly appreciated.

John graduated from AM&N College in 1968 and quickly moved into the music scene in Chicago. He would come back to campus periodically and check on us and sit in with the band. Being immersed in the Chicago music, he developed in the AACM and the "free-style" music. One night at a basketball game at the college, John cued the band and told us at his signal everyone should play free. That was new and different for all of us. We did it, but everybody really did not want to do it. Mr. Strong, our director, stood up, turned around, and looked as us—I do not recall his response, but we played free!

Back in 1977, I waved John to come and join the Duke Ellington orchestra at Disneyland. That was a great experience for us to play there at that time. By that time, John was many years experienced in New York City, teaching at colleges, performing worldwide as well as recording. He had his own agenda and projects. A well-assured and self-sufficient musician, he declined the invitation.

At the music educators national conference in Chicago in 1968 or 1969, John was applauded by Ms. Florence Bowser, an Afro American woodwind instructor for his timely commentary regarding "The contribution of Afro American Woodwind Players."

As for AM&N College, it was truly the experience of a lifetime to be among the many music students who studied and participated in music at the university level in Pine Bluff. Among them, John, Sonelious Smith, Larry Ross, James Leary, and I came together in The New Directions band. A few other people I must mention who saw John and all of us were Lawrence A. Davis (Prexy), the president of the college, Mrs. Howard, the librarian, Mrs. Wiley, Chair of the Music Department, and a host of others. Together we worked together, studied, practiced, learned, and honed our skills and planned out our future in music.

David L. Jones

In 1980, I moved from Houston, TX, to attend Berklee College of Music in Boston, MA, with three of my former high school classmates—Frank Lacy (trombonist), Michael Lewis (trumpeter), and Wendell Brooks (tenor saxophonist)—to study jazz music and to become a professional in the realm. I began to buy as many jazz records as I could get my hands on. In Boston there were quite a lot of record stores that sold used LPs cheap. You could find LPs from $2.00 up to $5.00.

One day while browsing, I came across a John Stubblefield record entitled *Midnight Sun*. I had never heard of John prior to seeing this record, but it was the cover that caught my attention. Being a saxophone player, I wanted to know of and hear every player in the jazz industry.

I finished Berklee in 1984 and moved to New York in 1990. I had been hearing and seeing John's name about in various billings and articles and eventually had the pleasure of hearing him perform with Kenny Barron at a club called Sweet Basil. His spirit and sound totally blew me away. I LOVED his tone on soprano saxophone. It was deeply influencing to me. I'll never forget that sound.

In 1992, I joined the Mingus Big Band, which had started a residency at a club in the lower East Village called the Time Café. The big band played downstairs in a speakeasy called The Fez. I remember my first night playing the second alto saxophone chair on the gig. John was in the second tenor chair to my left. He was sort of co-leading the band, calling out audibles, guiding the band through certain cues and various sections of the tunes that we played. The first impression of John that night was that of a "general in command." His presence was like a force to be reckoned with. But when we got off the bandstand, he came up to me and said, "Man, I like your sound. I hear that Southern Soul"—which was totally different from what I expected. He was so kind and gentle of a spirit. Very affable. His true southern manners radiated through his spirit.

Fast forward to a European tour with the Mingus Band in the summer of 1993. I call it the "Gunslinging Birds Tour" because it was on that tour that we recorded that CD (the BEST Mingus Big Band recording, in my opinion). This tour was with an "All-Star" cast of musicians. I remember the tour started in France and had many memorable moments, but one that stood out to me in my memory was being on a bus driving to one of the cities in France for our next engagement. John had a bottle of wine, and we all were partaking in a "little taste" of the grapes. So at one point during the ride, John got up and started joking and walking up and down the aisle like a general shouting, "Men! Do not tarry! Push ahead and maintain your position!" (I'm paraphrasing.) "We must keep pushing forward! Do not tarry!" He kept it up for quite a bit, and we all started acting like solders. It was so funny, the way he was saying it and looking just like a general. We had so much fun on that bus ride.

So then we were in Amsterdam playing the North Sea Jazz Festival (actually in Den Haag), and it was there when I met John's girlfriend Katherine Gogel. A lovely person who had quite an impressive "first impression" on me. Her spirit was so calming and sweet and seemed to be like a perfect fitting glove for John. We had such a great time in the Netherlands.

Later we were in Nice in the south of France playing the Nice Jazz Festival. It was a great festival with many great artists on the lineup. After we left Nice, it was on to Studio Mirival in the mountains of France to record the "Gunslinging Birds" record. I remember that it was a "growling" three days of recording every day. Reflecting on one of those days in the studio, I was struggling with a difficult flute passage written on my part that challenged me to play notes on my flute at the very top of the range of the instrument, and I had to play notes for a long duration (which was pretty challenging). I was also struggling because I wasn't quite sure of the fingering on how to play a high C at the extreme top range. I was sitting next to John and I leaned over and whispered to him, "Hey, man, how do you finger a high C?" He was so nice and said, "I believe the fingering is like this." I was so grateful—partly because I was embarrassed not to know and also because most of the other guys in the saxophone section were so, in my view, "big headed and conceited" that they would have frowned on me. But John was so cool and affable that I felt more comfortable asking him and knew that he would not "vibe" me.

After the tour ended and we returned to NYC, we resumed our weekly residency at the Time Café every Monday night, and the excitement picked up where it left off. Subsequently, I specifically remember on one of those Monday nights we were in between sets and a few of us were standing around the bar with John and I noticed that John's mood was different. It was as if he was troubled about something. It was a few weeks later it was revealed that he was in the hospital dealing with prostate cancer.

Wendell Jones

How did I meet John? Well you don't meet your next door neighbor/friend/brother whom you knew for 55 years. We automatically became a part of each other's life and shared many experiences together.

My first impression of John was that he was just like his dad. We called his dad the "crazy inventor." John's dad was a diesel mechanic, and he designed his personal workshop underneath the house where he created what he needed when he needed it. He could repair a car in a heartbeat. Whatever tool he needed, he made it, and when he made it, it worked.

John always tried to invent or build something. He was kind hearted, soft spoken, and determined to accomplish whatever he set out to do. I witnessed that in his music accomplishments. Well, he did invent something. He created his own music style.

I can remember so many days of what I called loud noise coming from next door. He practiced all the time! Little did I know that the loud noise he continuously made would turn into music that would be heard all around the world. I am honored to have grown up with John and to have been a part of his life. He represented his neighborhood, community, schools, the city of Little Rock and the state of Arkansas very well.

The last time I saw John was at his 60th birthday party in New York City at the home of Sue Mingus. Musicians filled the room that night in honor of John. There he was, the same John I had always known. I would like the world to know again that John was a kind-hearted, soft-spoken, and determined person who lived and loved music. I would like the world to remember that John never had a negative comment about anyone. He put all his time and efforts into music and was a powerful musician. The world and his neighbor/friend/brother miss him, but his music lives on.

Madeline Kamber

I first met John in 1970 at the Montreux Jazz Festival. I visited the festival with a girlfriend and we spent a week there. Something happened to me that had *never* happened before. We were standing at the bar in front of the concert hall, and on the other side of the bar I saw a man talking with friends. I looked at him for a while and told my friend, Esther, "If this man would get around me, I would be lost." Seemingly, he realized I was looking at him, only looking, not smiling, or similar. He then came over and said hello and asked me if I would come to the concert later. He said he would be playing in the Gil Evans Band. I said yes, and he then asked if we could meet afterwards, which we did. We walked along the shore of the lake and talked about who we were. I loved his playing, and he realized that I was a real music lover, mainly jazz. After a few hours we left each other, exchanging some kisses on the lake shore. I told John I would go back to Basel, Switzerland, the next morning, and he asked me for my address and said he would call me the following day. He had a day off and he decided to come to Basel and visit me. He arrived in the late afternoon and stayed until the following day … and there it happened.

When the Gil Evans Band returned to Europe, they were in Italy. I travelled for some days with John and the band. This was very precious for me because I had the opportunity to meet personally the other musicians with whom I am still in contact.

John and I stayed in close contact with phones and letters when I went to New York. Although I lived in Switzerland, I visited New York routinely every two years. We met again and had good times, visited with the many musicians. There was a residential place shared by musicians, artists, and others in the entertainment business, and this is where I met Fred Hopkins and other interesting people like James Baldwin. We also went out together to clubs and various other places. I recall during one of our visits together, I was told off specifically because I was white. I was told I had nothing to do there because I was not African American. John defended me, and then we left the place. This was a very important occasion for me to realize what it means and how much it touches people not to feel welcome in a society. I knew about the bad situation in Africa since I was a little child—when I heard that some Black people do not have enough to eat and die of hunger. This has always accompanied my life, and I am still very engaged for more justice in the world for all.

John had many LPs, but when he wanted to play something for me during our teaching sessions where I learned a lot about music, he could never find the LP on the shelf. So one afternoon I spent about two hours or more setting them on the shelf in alphabetical order. When he saw I had done this, he was very pleased with my idea and help.

I very much loved his saxophone playing and his compositions. It was often that he sent me cassettes with new songs or recordings from the gigs in the clubs. The music was alive and lush, and he would talk to me on these cassettes. I have his voice in my apartment because of course I kept them and I play them sometimes. On one of the cassettes, he plays "Midnight over Memphis," and he told me he would like to dedicate this composition to me. I am not a musician, except that I played Brazilian percussion instruments, and therefore cannot say clever things about his music. However, what I know is that his sound touched my soul and I know that he touched not only my soul, but also the souls of other listeners as well.

John was recently divorced when I met him. Afterwards, he was living with a partner, who I met, but I do not recall her name. She too was a musician. Along the way, John and I once talked about the possibility to move together, but I did not want to move to New York and I did not really want to become the partner of a musician who was always on tour here and there and meeting many groupies, of course. By the way, I never considered myself a groupie. It was nice to talk to musicians and learn about them and their lives, but I did not want to get involved with them after an event. John and I had a different relationship, and it could not be compared with that of a groupie. At that time, I had a partner too. Later we separated, and then I met Rudy, my husband, to whom I am still married. Rudy and I travelled to New York and visited John when he was in the extended care home. John had been ill for a while when we were finally able to visit him.

Toward the end of John's life he was in Calvary Hospital in the Bronx. I visited him there several times, and this is where I first met his sister, dear Joyce. I remember two special occasions from there. Once when I came, I thought everybody seemed so nervous. I asked what had happened, and they told me that President Bill Clinton had just left the hospital and had visited John. Both Bill Clinton and John were from Little Rock. I have photographs of Bill Clinton standing in front of John's bed. The other experience was on the bus en route to visit John. An Afro-American man in a wheelchair was on the bus. We left the bus at the same place, and I thought he must also be a patient because he did not look very well. After a while, as I sat at John's bed, the door opened and this same man came in. It was Dewey Redman, who was also a fantastic saxophone player.

One last experience, I called John on the phone from Switzerland and I could hear him breathing, but he did not say one word. I believe it was Joyce who said, "He feels very bad today." Later I heard that I was the last person to talk to him on the phone. This was very touching.

Jimmy Katz

I met John at Birdland through Joanna Ash, a friend of John's. Joanna was a well-known painter at Birdland. I told her I wanted to meet some musicians, and she introduced me to John and we hit it off right away. Not sure why so quickly, but we both were open and we had a lot of the same references in the jazz world. Joanna painted John on several occasions.

What I liked about John was that he had a unique sound and concept. He was warm and generous. I sort of judge musicians by who they are playing with. Musicians get validated by who they play with, and John was always playing with the best ones. If musicians play with people who you have never hear of, you do not know their true ability. John was playing with the best people on the scene at the time. This was my first impression of John and how I thought of him as a musician.

I recall John introduced me to the owner of Enja records, which allowed me to start working for their record label. While we were together one day, he said, "I will introduce you to the owner of Enja Records, Matthias Winckelmann." This was incredibly generous for him to do.

In many ways John was responsible for helping me get my foot in the door with jazz. John, Arthur Taylor, Eddie Henderson all introduced me to other musicians, and they were very supportive.

I got along with them all very well, understanding each of their different ways. We all clicked and had lots of fun.

When photographing John, we would have so much fun I would have to remind him we had to stop and take some pictures. I told him, "We can't just hang out. We have to take some pictures." It was fun to laugh and joke around and talk about things going on in the world. He would tell me things; he was the wisdom in the conversation.

John was a star soloist. I recall he performed a lot of solos with the Mingus Band. He also did a lot of work with Kenny Barron and McCoy Tyner.

John was really a wonderful person, and I will always feel fortunate to have known him. He was someone who wanted to have a positive impact on the world, and he was a warm, giving guy who understood to be a great artist in the jazz world one must play original music. This is how I remember John and I hope the world remembers him in this same way.

Boris Kozlov

I remember very well when I met John. It was either 1992 or 1993. I met him at a club named Vision near the Blue Note. Twice a week they had jam sessions at this club and tons of people would stop by. I had heard John's name before when he was with Kenny Barron and the Fort Apache Band. John was playing somewhere in the area that night, and he had stopped by for the jam session. Monday night was a big hang for most musicians. These were high level jam sessions—it was truly a professional thing. John had stopped by to say hi to Eddie Henderson whose band was the house band at the Vision. That same evening Junior Cook walked into the session. I was fairly new to the United States, and my English was not at full capacity at the time. I am a bass player and I can remember John was gracious and beautiful, and he complemented me on how I played. I later joined the Mingus Band in 1998.

My first impression of John was that he was really kind. I was a completely new face, a foreigner with an accent, and he was friendly to me. John made friends everywhere with people from every walk of life throughout the world. He had a presence about him. People would respect him at first glance.

He was one of the best-dressed guys in the Mingus Big Band. He was concerned about how we presented ourselves as band members. He would tell us, "We can do better than this. Look inside your wardrobes." He would do this in a respectful way, not to put anyone down but for us to think about how we were presenting ourselves to our audience. He had a lot of respect for the stage and audience. We called him the Chief of Intelligence. John came from the generation of musicians who were older and who were well dressed for a performance. My generation was used to playing in sneakers and shorts. When John was younger, the masters had a code of dress, and John got that code and passed it on to us. You never saw him without a jacket on stage. It was all about respect.

John was an incredible musician. He knew so much music. He knew how to wait a few moments to solo when playing. You knew that when John played a solo, that would be the climax of the set. It was pivotal. As young musicians, Jonathan Blake and I started to understand how to accompany that type of playing—the picture of that approach to playing became brighter and clearer. Musically speaking, John had so much information, he could create things. One night he might sound like Wayne Shorter, another John Coltrane, and John would say, "It's all in the blues." I often heard him say his biggest influence was the Chicago blues scene. John was one of the few who actually played with Mingus. He said Mingus was the first to give him a break when he arrived in New York.

I remember John would always have little packages of food with him everywhere he went. He told us that Junior Cook would say, "Always carry a sack." John would make a serious face and recite that proclamation. People now make fun of me because I take food away for events for the next day. Now I too always have a sack. Once while on a European bus tour, it was time for us to stop and eat. We stopped at a small place that did not offer a full meal. I remember John saying, "What kind of food is that? I have that kind of food in my sack."

Speaking about music, I was starting to act as the musical director for the Mingus Band. I felt shaky doing this, you know telling the band members what to play, etc. Once and a while I would put a set together and run it by John. He would make a recommendation if I questioned two blues sections together, but he would say there is nothing wrong in presenting the music this way.

I recall when John Stubblefield was the manager of the band and our piano player, John Hicks, joined us while we were on the road. John Hicks had come from another gig in the states and upon arrival in Europe he had not slept in 24 hours. Upon his arrival, we were off to play in London. Hicks was very tired and overslept and was not ready when it came time to catch the bus. John, as road manager, made it a point to knock on everyone's door to make sure everyone was ready. When he discovered that John Hicks was not ready, he got the key to his room, packed his bags, and made sure he would not be late. Whether road manager or not, John would make sure everyone was ready. John in his scripture reading voice would say, "No, we leave no man behind."

On my first tour, we went to Arizona. We were playing a large work written by Mingus called "Cumbia and Jazz Fusion." In that poetry was a chant that went "Mama's little baby don't like shorten bread. Mama's little baby like caviar, truffles, and the finer things in life." John would speak these pieces of poetry as we played. The next day we were getting on the bus in preparation to leave, and John was late getting on the bus. When he did arrive, Sue asked him, "Why are you late?" John responded, "Mama's little baby like breakfast."

I remember how John would greet everyone. I would say, "John, it is good to see you," and John would reply, "It is good to be seen." And this exchange would continue with a series of rhymes such as, "I know what you mean." He was full of wit.

Occasionally, during our many worldwide travels, we would get a day off. During that time, we would get on the bus and talk about what we did. Most of the band members would go sightseeing. Not John. I recall he would say, "I finished my Christmas shopping." John was always buying presents. He frequently bought presents for guys in the band. He would buy little things like handkerchiefs, jazz magazines, hats, etc. He loved giving presents.

Regarding gifts, I recall we were at the Red Sea Jazz Festival south of Israel, and one of the big features there were dolphins. People would go there to watch the dolphins, and they could swim with them, too. After our visit there, the next day when we got on the bus to leave, John showed us where he had bought a lot of dolphin souvenirs. He opened his bag and showed us all the different types of dolphins he had purchased. One of the band members was hung over, and John was worried that because there was a lot of tension in the area, if they found this band member inebriated, they might detain him. John said to him, "Look, man, you have to cool down because we are not going to leave you behind."

I recall if the music was not as it should be, John would pick a moment after the gig to talk to us about our playing, and this was done in a non-threatening way. If John ever had a fight with anyone, he would make up quickly. As musicians who traveled the world, we had long trips and they were tough. Mingus was known for setting musicians straight in his band. I remember once John had a disagreement with Phil Harper behind the stage before the performance began. The disagreement was over what song we would play first. A reporter in the audience overheard this and thought that the band was playing audio of Mingus speaking to motivate them as they went onto the stage. He would write in his article the next day that the Mingus Band was great inasmuch as they were still playing tapes of Mingus screaming at the band. Sue was elated this happened; she loved the publicity. I recall the next day John and Phil were fine. We stopped at the Auto Grill in Italy, and John bought lunch for Phil. At times, both John and Phil would laugh about that incident.

A lot of the music Mingus wrote was politically inspired. I was foreign born and did not know a lot about the politics of the United States. John would talk about things associated with the Civil Rights Movement. He would tell me that he lived that. He was the person who explained to me how America works. John was the biggest patriot of the United States. He would remind everyone of holidays and he celebrated and respected them. John was definitely a patriot.

John was the kindest guy, the greatest musician, super intelligent, and he made friends everywhere.

His musical legacy included working with many of the masters, e.g., Miles, Nat Adderley, Mingus Big Band, Kenny Barron , Fort Apache, his own band Quiet Fire. He was proud about his family. He talked about how many people in his extended family were musicians—I could tell when we talked, he was really proud. John was a peace maker in the band, if there was any kind of tension, he would address it by privately taking it away from the bandstand. It would get resolved. John was the heart of the Mingus Band and he is greatly missed.

Frank Kuumba Lacy

I had heard a lot about John—I had followed his music. I was going to school at Rutgers University in 1984. The head of the jazz department had been placed on hiatus, and John auditioned for the Jazz Professor position and was selected. This is the first time I met John Stubblefield, and he was my professor during 1984-1985. First, I was his student, and later we became best friends.

When I came to Rutgers, my expertise in music was ahead of many of my classmates. I was able to discuss jazz, arranging, improvisation, and other advanced aspects of jazz with John. I had studied at other highly specialized schools for music, including a bachelor of science at Texas Southern University and Berklee College of Music in Boston Massachusetts. John always liked me because he felt I was wise beyond my years. We would talk on the phone for hours. He used to tell me I was too smart for my own good. I told him that should not be a problem being a Black man in America.

Because he felt I was wise beyond my years, John and I were able to hang out personally and discuss music in great detail. My knowledge of music drew us closer together. I used music on a higher level, and he showed me things on a higher level. John and I became best friends. I called him "Prof." I would get mad at him and say, "F you, Prof," and he would say, "F you, Frank." It was just that way with us. Along the way, I think John kind of wanted me to stop calling him "Prof," but this is what I always called him, even until the time of his illness and transition.

I had a first impression of John long before I met him. It was kind of like meeting an idol, someone I always wanted to meet. Over the years, he was so down to earth, and he made me come down to earth and deal with him as a regular person. Everyone heard of John, the great John Stubblefield coming to teach at Rutgers, Wow! I had heard of him before I met him. I heard him play with Miles

Davis, the McCoy Tyner Big Band, and the Mingus Band. I heard his music—he was a legend before he came to teach us.

What made John such a great musician was his humanity. In many cases a musician's music is good, but most of those guys lacked humanity. John Stubblefield was like a regular person and a musician. Some of the other musicians were in obscurity, with attitudes, and not approachable. They were used to people kissing their ass all the time. Not John. He was not like that. He was approachable, a normal person, a regular guy. He would talk about sports and other things in life, ask about my family—just down to earth.

I remember once we had a two-hour layover in Houston, Texas, while traveling with the band. My mother and father had not seen me in a long time. My parents came to the airport to meet me, and John got off the plane and met my parents with me. I never met John's mother and father, but they raised him right.

Traveling with John was very interesting—I wish you could have heard him talk! He was like a jazz encyclopedia. The stores he told were incredible, and he kept the band's spirit high.

I remember my last tour with John and the Mingus Band. We were leaving the US traveling to Europe. John was walking slow, and I told the others I was going to walk slow with Prof. We got to the gate, and the band had left us. The airlines fixed us up on another flight, and John and I made the gig on time. This happened in 2004, and I thought it was wrong that they had gone off and left us. After all, John was the star of the band.

John was very particular about things, especially someone else carrying his horns. Those horns were delicate, and they could easily be damaged, so he preferred to carry his own horns. He was also very particular about the music—that was part of the genius about him.

I do not think many people know that John could have had a side job as a stand-up comic. Once we were in the South of France in Nice performing in the Nice Jazz Festival. While there, they had asked if we would do a set at the hotel where we were staying. During that set, John started talking, and for 20 minutes or more, he did stand-up comedy. It was hilarious!

I recall he kept the young musicians on their toes. Charles Mingus wrote over 300 songs, and John felt we should explore all the music, not just a few pieces of it. At this time, John was one of the oldest members of the Mingus Band. He had worked with Mingus, so he understood the intent of the music Mingus wrote and shared that with band members.

John lived for the music. He was rare. He understood humanity. He was a great musician, high level but a regular guy. He knew how to talk to people from all walks of life, yeah, he just talked to everyday people on the street. Watching John influenced me to be like that. I follow my artistic ability and humanity as a career like John. I emulate John in being a human being in this art form. He was the example of "good people." If he had a disagreement with you, he would call back and apologize. That is how men used to be—no grudges. This was John.

The Bible speaks of life everlasting. I found out in a class the memory of a person is life everlasting. It is the least common denominator; memory is electrical impulses in the brain. So the way I look at John Stubblefield, "Prof,"—he is still alive in me. Having been with John and shared so many experiences, yes, he is still with me. My father used to tell me, "Son, your close friends you can count them on one hand, and you still may have some fingers left. John was one of those friends I could count on one hand. More so than a musician, John was my friend. If he could not play the saxophone, he would have been my friend. Forget the music. The music was second. I am happy to say I knew John like that. A lot of the people we worked with would never look at you like a friend. I treasure that John Stubblefield looked at me like a friend. He was a real cat and good people.

John was a deep person.

James Leary

I met John at Booker T. Washington Elementary School in Little Rock in 1952. I was in the first grade, and John's brother, William, was in my class. John came to the room to bring William's lunch money. There was a special type of lunch going on that day. John was in the second grade.

As far as music was concerned, I knew he was in the band at Dunbar Junior High School when I got there. I knew John and his best friend, Mahlon Martin. When I arrived at Dunbar, I saw them all playing in the band. As I recall, John was playing clarinet, and Mahlon the trombone.

I always thought John was a good musician. He could read music. He used to test me to see if I could read the music he wrote—this went on for six or seven years. Later on when I started to understand how to play jazz, John would say it was not important to learn to play chord changes first. John Bush and I felt it was important to learn to play chord changes. John said we should just play and not learn chord changes. He just felt it was no need to learn the chord changes in the beginning. We were teenagers 16 years old having this discussion. Later, John did relent and learn the chords. John became a hell of a saxophonist. Troy Betton was a trumpet player and he was in one of York Wilburn's first bands. The group was called York Wilburn and the Thrillers, and John played with that band along with Troy, Robert Trezvant, and myself.

John was a year ahead of me. When I graduated high school, I went to North Texas State. John was in his second year at AM&N College when he told me that the band director, Harold Strong, wanted me to come to AM&N. When I left North Texas State, John talked to Mr. Strong and asked him to give me a scholarship to come to AM&N, and he did. I was working at a stationery store in

Little Rock on Main Street. When I found out I had received the scholarship, I quit my job and headed for "The Yard." (This is what students referred to AM&N College.) When I got to The Yard, the first place I stayed was in a dormitory; however, after school started, John went to Coach McPherson and requested that I move to the Red Barn and I did.

The Red Barn was a house made out of red boxcar wood. While living there we would play the music loud. The neighbors never complained, and I have no idea how they put up with the music. One night the man did come over, however, and told us to please turn the music down. We were surprised he put up with it as long time as he did.

While on campus I played in the jazz band The New Directions—Larry Ross (drums), Ben Jones (trumpet), Sonelius Smith (piano), John (sax), and me (bass). We played gigs on and off campus. There was a musician who lived in Pine Bluff who taught at Merrill High School. He used to turn the cats on to a lot of people. Sometimes he would book the band. He eventually joined AM&N's faculty and started the Jazz Band department. I cannot recall his name, but he was instrumental in getting us gigs with Solomon Burke, Johnnie Taylor, Major Lance, and others. John used to do a number of those gigs. Actually, Thomas East and John came to North Texas State while I was there. They were working on a gig with Solomon Burke.

Lawrence A. Davis was the President of AM&N College, and he was instrumental in getting The New Directions Jazz Band hooked up with the University of Indiana Jazz Festival. The first time we performed, we lost the competition, but we did come back later on and win. This was our first trip to Europe. We had some interviews with the *Pine Bluff Commercial* and the Little Rock newspapers because we had participated in these festivals. As a reward for winning, President Davis brought us all back to Pine Bluff for a concert on the yard. Back then, we did things beyond the music department. We did a lot of rehearsals on campus. At that time, the school did not have a jazz band, but John and I were so jazz-oriented, we prompted the school to get interested in having one. Years after graduation, Grace Wiley brought The New Directions Quintet back again for a reunion in1998.

While taking an orchestration class from Harold Strong, Stub somehow got a copy of the final exam. He told me this was the same test Harold Strong was giving everyone. In that moment Harold Strong was driving down the street. He recognizes the paper, stops his car, gets out and walks up to us, takes the paper, and tells us we will have to take the test again. It was actually the test that someone had already taken, but he was going to give us something different. We were given a new test. We just knew he was going to give us a super hard test, so we studied as hard as medical doctors. We passed!

I also recall John's mom, Mrs. Stubblefield, used to bring food by the Red Barn. She would drop by and bring some delicious food. I recall one time the neighbor got the food and thought it was for me. We had not been there, so she'd left it with the neighbor. The neighbor thought it was for me, so I started eating the food only to find out when John came home that the food was from *his* mom, not my mom, because my mom did not know where I lived. We were some of the hungriest people in the world. Nokie Taylor was one of our roommates and he was partially blind, but he could cook. I remember we went to the grocery store and some guys liberated some food. Ham in a trumpet case from the Mad Butcher. We liberated all this food we could get and we had a feast. We did not have any money and no food. We did not eat on campus. We lived off campus and made our own way. When we played for a dance, they had huge trays of food, and when the dance was over, we would carry the food home before we carried our instruments home. As I look back, there were several of us who lived in the Red Barn—Dewitt

Chapel, John, Nokie Taylor, Joe Gardner, and myself. All have transitioned except Nokie and myself.

The last time I saw John he was in the hospital. I was returning from a gig in Japan, and I was stopping in New York. I said, "Yeah, if I don't talk to this dude, he is going to kill me while in the hospital." We had a long visit, and while there we talked about my music, and he gave me advice on some new arrangements I was working on.

His works are recorded. He was a composer. He had a lot of friends and he knew a whole lot of people. Just regular people and musicians. His work stands on its own. Let him be judged by his work.

Jason Marshall

I first met John in Washington, D.C., at the Kennedy Center in 1999. Ronnie Cuber, a member of the Mingus Band, invited me to come hear them play. Ronnie Cuber and John played second tenor between the lead alto and baritone saxophone players. I was a young musician at the time with aspirations of one day moving to New York. This was my first meeting with John, and I remember him giving me his autograph on the program.

John's sound blew me away! The strength of his sound—it was easily identifiable. It was just that John's sound was so present. I was young and could not understand what was so transcendent about that sound. While there were a lot of strong musicians in Washington, D.C., I wanted to go to New York and play.

John's playing was informed music that was very resonate. When I heard John play, it reminded me of the blues and gospel I heard while growing up. His music was instantly relatable and very moving.

After meeting him in 1999, I did not see him again until 2003 when I moved to New York. He was still with the Mingus Band, but not long after that he was in a wheel chair.

I remember meeting John again at the Thyme Café. I would go every week to hear him play and bring my horn, hoping they would let me set in. I got to the club and John looked at me and said, "You look like you are ready to stand up and be counted." He was the first person to acknowledge me in that way. That statement always stuck with me. At the time, I was a student at the New School University. In New York everyone is trying to be somebody. Me, I just wanted the opportunity to "sit in."

The Black American Experience is very valid and worthy of attention and respect. John played the Black American Experience. He was very focused on the mission, not in an aggressive way but as a constant teacher and reminder of the Black experience. I have been with the Mingus Band steady since 2014. Most of the time I sit next to Abraham Burton who now sits in the chair where John sat. When we play, Abraham from time to time will say, "Man, I wish you could have played with John." I want people to remember how the music was an experience and John was grounded in that experience.

Andy McKee

I met John soon after I moved to the Lower East Side of Manhattan. John and I lived in the same neighborhood. The neighborhood was interesting because it had a large community of jazz musicians. Don Cherry, Cee Sharp (the alto player from Philadelphia), Dennis Charles, Steve Slagle, Jimmy Lovelace all lived there at that time. Joe Lee Wilson (the great vocalist from Oklahoma) had an "office" down a short set of stairs from the sidewalk on Fourth Street between First and Second Avenues. I became a regular there along with lots of the local jazz community who would stop by to catch up on all the latest jazz news. I met John for the first time during that period in the early 80s on a gig with Joe Lee somewhere in that Lower East Side neighborhood. I was playing in a lot of clubs in the city, and of course John and I would see each other from time to time. I'm remembering his place was on Ludlow Street down from Katz's Deli. Below Houston Street there were a number of those basement "office" spaces that many musicians rented for practice and rehearsals.

The things that struck me most when I first met John were his big personality and the quality of his musicianship. He had an individual voice on the saxophone.

John was a real professional—serious, and as I said, he really had his own voice on the saxophone. Many musicians hope to accomplish this inasmuch as it is not an easy thing to do. John accomplished it. He had a sound that was unique, a sound that exposed his spirit.

Thinking of John and his personality, this touching story comes to my mind. In the late 90s, perhaps 1997, the father of Dave Taylor, our bass trombone player, died while we were on tour in Europe. It was complicated, of course. Dave had to go home, and Earl McIntyre flew in to finish the tour with us. A week or two after we had returned to the city, I saw John in the neighborhood, and we had coffee together. While there, John pulled out a sympathy card to send to Dave Taylor. He asked me to sign the card with him to send to Dave. This was touching to me; I did not always think like that. It was so thoughtful on John's part. He was still thinking about Dave two weeks after the tour was over. Maybe one of the reasons I remember this so vividly is because I was a bit surprised with this side of John that I did not know before. We signed the card and sent if off. I have never forgotten that, it was so thoughtful.

Another thing that comes to mind is a tune we used to play with the Mingus Big Band called "Hog Callin' Blues." I'm smiling ear to ear now just thinking about it! In this piece, there was a long solo for the tenor player. This was the perfect vehicle for John to solo and express himself. Again, it was a long solo that was fun, and it

was a piece John totally owned. There was squawking and screaming like a hog. John would really dig into it. It was his piece. This
was recorded on one of the band's earlier recordings, *Gunslinging
Birds*. Somewhere along the line, I found a necktie with hogs on it
and gave it to John, and he totally cracked up! And more than once
donned the tie for our performance of "Hog Callin' Blues."

I also remember John was a member of the Fort Apache Band.
They did several recordings and toured as a working group. Their
music was amazing. This group was wide open, with fun and creative and serious music where John's contribution was substantial.

Lastly on February 6, 2020, I traveled along with Abraham
Burton and Helen Sung to the University of Arkansas at
Fayetteville to play a concert in honor of John. This event was held
to announce that the John Stubblefield Papers are now catalogued
and housed in the Special Collections division of the library at the
university. It was such a privilege to take part in this concert com-
memorating the life and legacy of my friend, John Stubblefield.
By all accounts it was a big success.

I want people to remember his spirit—his smile. I saw him
once while he was in the hospital near the end of his life. Even
in those difficult days he was still smiling and telling stories that
had visitors and hospital staff cracking up. His spirit was uplifting
and contagious.

Earl McIntyre

The first time I met John was at a rehearsal with Warren Smith
uptown in a building owned by the Collective of Black Artists
(CBA). The CBA put on large concerts in the city during that time.
I got a last-minute call to come and rehearse, and while there I met
John. This happened around 1973 when I was considered the baby
of the group (20ish). John and I were also subs with the Mel Lewis

Band. John and I played in the Mingus Band—John was already in the band when I got there. We played together for many years.

My first impression of John was that he was very settled, and I could tell he was very talented. New York was my home, the place where I grew up, attended school. It was a place with which I was very familiar. John was new not only to the group but also to New York City and took his time warming up. This was a good environment for John to begin to feel out New York and just check out different people. Just like most new musicians as they arrive in New York, it took time to blend into the environment. After that, we were just one big family.

John was a really dedicated musician. He connected the dots where a lot of people do not. He had one foot in the Avant Garde era and the other in the Blues. His music was both in the tradition and in the future. He had a lot of latitude in his concept of music. He could easily transcend into a lot of different musical styles. He played with a lot of great people, and he picked up a lot from them. In a sense John was an under-rated player—but well-seasoned by playing with the Masters. He was a team player. He was always concerned about the team. I miss that from John. Now, it appears young players can only think about how their solos went.

Once while playing in San Francisco, we had several young players and they were into their own time. They liked to start and dissolve the music like Miles Davis in the mid-60s. I remember while we were playing at Yoshie's, John stood up and said to the youngsters, "Gentlemen, we are playing the music of Charles Mingus, not Miles Davis in the 60s," and then he sat down. This statement from John really changed their attitudes.

Often when things would go awry in the band, John would say or do something to get the ship to go in the right direction. It was not a nasty or take-over type of thing. It was "this is the way the music is supposed to go," and it made a difference in the way the band functioned.

The BLUES! Whatever he played, he played the blues. That was always the backdrop for John. He was a gentleman; old-school jazz musicians were like that. John was one of the last of that school in some ways. He was a brilliant musician in many ways, and the color he painted always favored the blues. No matter what, his go-to thing was to play the blues. He could make it be what was necessary for the moment. He had his own way of expressing himself verbally. These are some of the things for which we should remember John.

I came to a gig where John was playing in Nate Adderley's Band along with Buddy Williams, Onaje, (Allan Bentley Gumbs), and Fernando Gumbs. While John's primary horn was the tenor saxophone, this night he was playing his soprano saxophone. While he was playing, I noticed he was turning his head from left to right with each breath taken. I told him he sounded great but asked him why he kept turning his head from side to side. He then replied that he was swimming to improve his breath control. He was using the swimming technique as he blew his horn that night. He always thought different.

I recall Onaje was on the phone all the time. John decided to invite us to his apartment on Ludlow to celebrate Onaje's birthday. I remember John had an entire wall covered with some scales he was trying to master. At this party we did a roast for Onaje, and we all had phones.

John was losing his hair, and he found out my wife was making hair cream. They talked, and Rene would make this cream for John to use on his scalp.

One other thing that happened, I wrote a piece for another organization called the Musicians of Brooklyn Initiative—an organization started by Lester Bowie and Oliver Lake. This was a special event to be held at the Town Hall in Manhattan. This concert was performed by a 40-piece band plus a soloist. The words were written by Paul Lawrence Dunbar, and one of the featured soloists was John. John loved playing with a large ensemble. I became interested in Paul Lawrence Dunbar because so many jazz musicians who came from down South would frequently recite his poems. It is with that research and inspiration I wrote the music.

On our last tour to Europe, I could tell there was something wrong with John. I remember helping him with his horns and luggage. As I think of this, it still tears me up. John looked at me and said, "If I ever did anything to hurt you, I apologize." I will forever remember that.

Wilford (Jackie) Moore

[I wrote this account after hearing of Dr. Moore's transition, Joyce.]

I received Dr. Moore's response to my interview questions on October 31, 2021. In December, I received an email informing me that he had passed away at 7:41 p.m. on December 7, 2021. Jackie was a renaissance man who was both kind and brilliant. I know John felt the same way. Jackie was like a brother to him, and they were like-minded intellectuals in their discussions about life, music, education, and many other aspects of life. They understood the "vibes."

I met Jackie for the first time as he sat by my brother's bedside when John was hospitalized in New York Presbyterian Hospital. Jackie made several visits to be by John's side during the period from April 2004 to July 2005. John had spoken to me about Jackie often, and I was glad to actually meet him.

Jackie said he met John about 1959. He said John was terrific. Jackie said that John was like a brother to him. Around 1979, John left New York City for a year and lived in California with Jackie. At that time, John was going through a divorce and separated from his son, John C. As Jackie explained, John's time in California was time to heal. Jackie's son was inspiration as John worked through the healing process of the divorce and separation from John C. After about a year of readjusting, John decided to return to New York, and he remained there until his transition on July 4, 2005.

John and Jackie remained in constant contact. Only someone as close as a brother would do this. Jackie stated that John was a good arranger and an excellent composer. He further stated he and John were at their best when they were playing music together. You see, Jackie played tenor sax also. Finally, Jackie said John was one of the finest musicians he had the pleasure to know and to play music with.

Amina Claudine Myers

I met John, whom I called Stub, while attending Philander Smith College in my senior year. I recall my sorority Delta Sigma Theta was having our annual Delta Ball, and we were under the impression that Arthur Porter, another local musician, was going to provide the music for this event. Arthur Porter sent Stub over to play for us, and we had an attitude because Art Porter did not come. Before the night was over, we had respect for John and the band because they could play.

The group turned out to be very warm. I remember one other member of the group was Henry Shead. I had not met anyone else other than professional people prior to meeting John's group— they were up and coming. This was my first impression of Stub, and this is how we became friends. They were handling the music that night. When Stub played, he had his own style. He could play anything and was serious about his music. The next time we met was in Chicago. I taught school in Chicago and was a member of the Association for the Advancement of Creative Musicians (AACM). Stub joined the AACM while living in Chicago.

Stub was a Master Musician. He saw something in me long before I saw it in myself.

I remember when Stub's son, John, was four years old, he spoke like an adult. There was a statement he made that was ridiculously cute. I cannot recall it now but it was far beyond his age.

I remember while John was living in Chicago, his instruments were stolen. I know he was hurt over that incident.

I recall once we were on a double-decker bus touring and Stub was upstairs. He called downstairs to the bus driver and asked me to come up where he was. We enjoyed the view from the upper deck together.

Stub had come into the recording studio with me as I wanted to take a quartet to Europe. We made a recording to send to the promoters. We did not get the job, and later Stub transitioned. I visited John while he was in the nursing home on 70th Street, and I saw him in Calvary Hospital in the Bronx where a nurse was with him 24 hours.

I remember once we were on the road with Charley Haden. We went to a restaurant in the hotel in France, and Stub went back in the kitchen with the chef. Stub was on a roll cooking breakfast with the chef. Stub had invited himself into the kitchen and that was that.

Stub used to play my piano so hard that it would be out of tune when he played it. I would say, "Stub don't play so hard. My strings are old."

Stub turned me on to some great artists' music and I still have that music along with a song he wrote for me entitled "Dino." Only one other person called me that, a close teacher friend of mine. I still have that song in my material, and I am going to play it.

After I moved to NYC, Stub invited to his home for dinner. A great home cooked meal by his wife. I was honored. That was a nice gesture on his part. He is the one who was responsible for me becoming a jazz messenger. I believe Art Blakey was looking for a pianist. Stub kept up with the music scene. Stub gave me updates on working with Art, and that was a success.

Stub was a well-known and beautiful musician; he was a master. He was well-respected and understood his craft. He could play anything. He understood music. Stub had his own thing going on—he was funny. Stub was just Stub. He was very soulful, and he had a big sound. He was a sweet person, a very warm and loving individual. And Stub Loved Music!

I want the world to remember that John Stubblefield was a very warm person who had an understanding of many styles of music and was able to play them all. He was serious, and music was all he spoke about when I was around him. He would sit at the piano working on a new composition. He was soulful, and one could hear his soulfulness in his playing. He was considerate of people's feelings and could see their makeup, being an artist who could see inside one's mind. In some cases, I believe he knew who they were before they did. He was a quiet man who continued listening and studying the masters—constantly growing. He developed his creativity, including a big warm sound on the tenor sax. I knew him as an artist who would help you when he could, never saying no. I will always remember him for his artistic abilities and his beautiful soul.

Aklaff Pheeroan

I don't remember how I met John. I'm not sure why I don't remember. Especially since he played such a pivotal role in my life and career. Maybe it was in a large ensemble, or maybe he asked me to play a concert with him. The only thing I remember is that Clint Houston played bass with us. If that is the case, it was certainly a gig that paid off in grater ways, because he played the cassette tape for Tom Pierson. Tom was able to convince me that I could actually play his music because he heard that tape. And he knew that if John thought well of me, then he would have no problems. It was one of the most fortuitous recommendations I had ever had and resulted in my friendship with the most important orchestrator and big band composer I have worked with.

My first impression was that John was kinder than any of the Miles Davis alums I had ever met, forged but not tainted from that tenure. His generosity was equal to his genius. As a fellow Aquarian, he understood my true desire to play deep and important music, without boundaries of genre and devoid of posturing that came along with many, especially horn players.

I respected his work so much that I sheepishly asked him if he would, one, play with me in a quartet with Jerome Harris on electric bass and Rob Schwimmer on keyboards, and two, if we could play one of his compositions.

We were also playing "The Three Marias" and "Endangered Species" from Wayne Shorter's Atlantis record, and I thought John would enjoy being highlighted in this way. After all, I never forgot how lucky I was to have him on the bandstand.

Well actually there was one time I did forget. When I asked everyone if they would wear a band shirt I had designed, John memorably said, "I don't mind wearing one of your shirts, but yellow? Why would you want us to wear yellow shirts. That is the worst color." I knew he was the best tenor player I could have the fortune of being associated with. He made my playing expand and mature. He gave my young quartet distinction.

Regret is useless, but it is appropriate sometimes. Many of us wish that John could have gotten more recognition, if that is even a rewarding thing. I'm not sure that he gave as much to himself as he did to others. It's just something that you can tell sometimes. His comportment was of a signature style and grace that moved easily into his telling the history of our people through his horn. He always struck me as a gentleman with distinction who indulged my raucous development. I'll never forget how gracious he was to my friend Veronica Nunn when he found out she was from Little Rock. And neither one of them struck me as Southerners until they were in the same room. And then of course his sense of humor. I'll never forget how much enjoyment he got from flipping the light switch in my apartment and saying "Keep the light on." The switch plate was a smiling clown. And of course, the switch poked out of the clown's pants zipper.

John had many musicians who respected his gifts. He also shared wisdom with burgeoning players like me. Once he said to me something quite memorable when it took me a while to pay him for a job I was underwriting. "Well, Pheeroan, you don't want to die owing people money." That's such a good line that I never repeated it.

John played on the only tour I had in Europe, which was only three gigs: the Willisau Concert, a little concert space in Chur (Switzerland), and the Unterfahrt Club (Germany), and on the Sonogram CD. He gave my crude etchings mature sonority and sophistication, contributed one of his own compositions to our book, and took all of the repertoire beyond our imagination.

Michael Rabinowitz

I met John when I went down to hear the Mingus Big Band at the Time/Fez Café. We spoke and I remember his presence in the band.

John was very supportive and encouraging to me. I played in the Mingus Orchestra, but not with John. I played the bassoon, an instrument that carries a different sound. John would say positive and complimentary things about my playing, and this helped me along. While John had strong opinions and suspicions about things, I always respected him and had a good feeling about him and how he carried himself in the band.

I did not hear John a lot, but when I did hear him play, it was with great passion and intelligence.

I recall there were some pieces that Mingus had written that were specifically about racism. I recall John speaking up and making it known to the band that Mingus was making it clear that America was racist and the music was written in protest of that.

John would at some points do a soliloquy reminding the band members of the intent of the piece being played. The fact that John was outspoken about this on the bandstand sticks in my mind.

John was the heart of the band. I remember Sue saying when John transitioned that it was tough on the band. He had been there from the beginning and was a key element to the band. He had strong emotions, and that flowed through the band. I remember it was tough on a lot of people when John died.

John was a very generous person, dedicated and passionate about life, and that extended to the music he played. While we did not play together frequently, I think of John this way: sometimes when you do not have a close relationship with someone, the glimpses from afar are profound. John expressed the emotion of the Mingus Band.

Kenny Rampton

I met John while playing in the Olivier Gatto band in Boudeaux, France. Olivier used to put together groups of his friends and other legendary musicians to play in France. I first met John on a flight to France to play in one of those gigs. I knew who he was and was blown away sitting in his presence. There he was, sitting next to me. He was sitting in his seat writing music while waiting on the plane to leave.

During our initial meeting, we found ourselves in a holding pattern on the plane from New York City to Paris. On this flight, the takeoff was delayed for some reason and it was very uncomfortable sitting there in the hot plane. People were sweating, hot, and ready to leave. My first impression of John was during this time when everyone was frustrated and stressing out. I watched him deal very calmly with this adversity in a graceful way. He just sat there and wrote music. This was my first impression. John was calm, and this taught me a valuable lesson as a young musician. I will always remember how he was patient and graceful under pressure. I always wanted to be around John.

He was a brilliant musician. You hear a lot of jazz music on stage now, and it sounds as if they are practicing. John was always expressing his deepest feelings when he played. He was always connecting with a high power and the people. He played very raw, and he had an amazing technique. He got on stage and expressed himself. He was a master at doing that. I loved his playing so much. His sound was beautiful, wide open and incredible—just like his mind and his heart.

I can only think of two saxophone players similar to John—John Coltrane and Wayne Shorter. John mastered the saxophone and achieved that kind of tone on the sax, the same kind of quality they had. As I recall, John and Wayne Shorter were friends.

Along with his passion for music, John was deeply interested in things that go beyond music. He shared a lot of interesting subjects with me. He read a lot, and he encouraged me to read books like *The Shadow Government, Behold the Great White Horse*, etc. It is very interesting that a lot of information discussed in those books is happening right now.

John set a standard of dress for the musicians. He was dressed nice all the time. We really had not given it much thought. Most of us would show up in jeans and tee shirts. He wanted everyone to look sharp and wear jackets. The jeans and tee shirts were just too casual. He persisted and everyone began to dress differently. We got to set the standard a little bit higher. Everyone began to wear jackets, but I did not have a jacket, so John gave me one of his to wear. We were always curious about the music and wanted to present ourselves in the highest levels when we performed. John wanted everyone to reach the highest level of integrity.

John was an expert in music. While sitting in front of the brass section, he would turn around and make the "Wa" sound. Also, I remember sitting in the saxophone section with the trombone players behind us. We had to deal with getting hit by the slides, and at the end of the valves there were spit valves. As John would say, "We got hit and spit" and "the fight has not friends." He would say this a lot.

Just before we would go on stage for a jazz festival, he would say, "All right, gentlemen, let's leave some blood on the stage." He had all sorts of funny sayings that kept us moving. Once on a long bus ride, He was walking up and down the aisles talking about different things such as Yin and Yang. He had a way of saying things that was just hilarious.

He had incredible integrity and a passion for life and music. I do not know if he thought of himself as an educator, but he was one of my greatest teachers. He led by example. He was a true artist in every sense of the word. He was the heart and soul of the band. Everyone will say the same thing. Since he left, the band has never been the same for me. He bonded with the spirit of Charles Mingus. Through his examples we all learned so much.

Mike Richmond

I met John in the early-to-mid 80s at a gig in New York. Jazz bands were being displayed from around the world at this venue. The club was called the Knitting Factory, and I was there playing base and John saxophone.

He was 100% aware of the history of the music. Not every-one spends the time to do that. He was a great player, an overall encompassing musician. He had those musical qualities. It was great to know someone who was so sensitive to the band. It goes beyond being a great saxophone player. He had great musical instincts. He did not just play a great solo, he heard what the other musicians were playing, too. When you do a solo, you are responding to all of the other instruments in the band. John had "big ears." This enabled him to hear himself and others play.

He was always very musical. He knew the history of what he was doing. He was 100% Coltrane. In his early stages, you could tell he listened to Pharaoh Sanders. We were closer to the 50s, 60s, 70s era of music, but John was aware of what had gone on earlier—music played by the masters. You could hear that in his solos and his tone. With the Mingus Big Band, it was good to be familiar with the older bands (e.g., Louis Armstrong, Count Basie, etc.). Great saxophone players played in these historical bands, and John knew all about them. Much of Charles Mingus' music touched the older music. "Jelly Roll," written by Mingus, was a tribute to Jelly Roll Morton. You have to know that style, and this is what John studied. It was not possible to play authentically without knowing that. John knew that and you could hear it in every note and phrase.

I was impressed that John listened to everyone. We listened to other musicians' recordings, but John listened to the base lines and melodies that other players played. He listened to all the melodic lines and played along with that. As a bass player, I looked forward to working with people who listened. John did that, and I was always impressed with his ability to listen.

When we played, he was always swinging really hard. In jazz we play the swinging eighth note, and John knew how to swing with that.

I remember when John was putting his albums together, he put great musicians together. He knew how and who to choose the musicians to produce the sound he wanted to produce. It was like assembling a team for a government office, selecting the right people to make sure the work gets done.

Soulful.

Scott Robinson

John Stubblefield was a true original—a deep thinker, someone who had his own way of looking at everything—and it showed in his music. He got better with age, and those who were fortunate enough to hear him play live know that his recorded oeuvre only hints at the breadth and depth of what he could do. John's playing somehow effortlessly combined the traditional and the avant garde, along with his own unique energy and spirit—and through it all ran those deep twin rivers, the Tigris and Euphrates of our music: Soul and the Blues.

He was always an encouraging and friendly force who took a genuine interest in what his colleagues were up to, whether or not they were as respected and experienced as he was. I was still pretty green when I first got to know him, but he always made me feel like a player he respected and cared about. We would trade albums occasionally, and he would really listen to what I gave him and show real enthusiasm for it later. It was my honor to play music with John, and to sub for him on a number of occasions with the Mingus Band. Big shoes!

For me, Stubbs was a real model of how to always be yourself as a player while also meeting the needs of the music at all times. Like other masters of our artform, he was highly expressive and individualistic, taking liberties, but also giving to the big picture. This is the balance creative music demands, a balance not everyone manages to strike.

I visited John in the hospital during his final illness and was struck by how he maintained his positivity and work ethic during that most difficult time. He carefully and enthusiastically explained to me his exercise regimen, how he had measured the room he was confined to and figured out how many times he had to crisscross it in order to walk X number of miles per day. While I wasn't too sure about his math, I marveled at how matter-of-factly he faced his illness and what he needed to do to remain productive. He proudly showed me three or four arrangements he was working on for the Mingus Band, intricate constructions meticulously rendered with pencil and paper—joyful, final works he knew would outlive him and thata are, indeed, still played by the band today. It was a special pleasure, in fact, to play a couple of these for his sister Joyce in Arkansas while on the Mingus Centennial Tour that I am returning from today as I write this on the airplane.

John Stubblefield is one of the people I wish I had made more time for, gotten to know better, while I had the chance. But I will always feel fortunate to have known him, and heard him, and played music with and by him. He continues to inspire me, and I feel his presence. A spirit like his does not just depart this world so easily, or so completely.

Michele Rosewoman

People got happy when they ran into Stubb.

He seemed to be taking in everything around him all the time. Whatever he was in the midst of, his attention and respect stayed fully with whoever he was talking to, but at the same time he somehow fully acknowledged your presence. His eyes invited you over—as well as perhaps an outreached hand—while his other hand would reach out and touch whoever he was talking to so that his transitions were seamless. He connected everything up. He left no one out. I can see his face, his eyes, his manner as I write this.

There was humor and mischief in his eyes most all of the time that I saw him in public. He was one of the most social people I knew. He had everyone going—laughing and feeling good. The Gov'nor. A diplomat—of sorts. Behind closed doors, another thing at times. So I hear.

He came to PLAY and he came to PLAY.

In my early days in New York, we somehow met. I can't remember the context, but we were just suddenly musically involved. He was open and willing, and was one of the first established musicians to support and contribute to my efforts and outcomes. He looked for assurances and when he got them, he went head on. Stubb was a member of my 14-piece New Yor-Uba ensemble when we debuted in 1983 at the Public Theatre. In 1984 we went on a three-week tour to Europe. Here are some of the things I remember about John on that tour:

- We were on a bus driven by a German bus driver, and we were his worst nightmare—a diverse, stylized bus full of expressive musicians. We put music on—whatever we felt like hearing, turning each other on to different things. One evening when were all tired and nodding, the bus driver put on his own music. John yelled from the back of the bus, "Turn that s—t off!" We all couldn't help but laugh, and that racist bus driver had no choice. We ran the show.

- Stubb had a theme back then—"Drink up and BE somebody!" A mixed message but we had to laugh. One of my dear friends and ensemble members, now gone, had a real drinking problem. He was very sensitive, and drinking made it worse. Someone came to my room and told me, "Eddie is downstairs crying." He had broken down crying because an Austrian that he thought he was communicating with gave him a Heil Hitler salute, and it took him out. I went downstairs where some of the musicians along with John were surrounding him, trying to console him. Stubb was leading the way.

- After leaving gray Warsaw where he was put out of the hotel for exchanging money on the black market and getting busted—Stubb was lit up when we got to Zurich, which was full of life, color, and energy. He said, "The first woman I see in black stockings is in trouble." When a good friend of mine walked into the dressing room to greet me, I said to myself (and maybe to others) "Uh oh." He got his way on that one. He was a charmer.

Soon after we were back in New York, I was disappointed when he couldn't make my thing (an important thing!) because he got the gig with Freddie Hubbard. I didn't like many horn players' sound on soprano and didn't know what to do. But I just went on, got happy for him, and got guided to good things that led to more good things.

So many years later, I visited him at the hospital. He was not in his room—had guests and was in a visiting room where he had the whole place laughing. He grabbed all of us and took us downstairs to a room with a piano. Folks started making music. The nurses said he was always on the move, kept them laughing, and had an endless stream of visitors. I'm glad I was one. He was still joyous and spreading joy. He still had hope then and was still just living life.

But the sad times eventually came, and my two visits to John at hospice were emotionally challenging. I felt his anger at his circumstance—he was not in a state of acceptance. It was too soon, too unexpected, impossible to believe. He didn't really look us in the eyes. He had no patience for uncomfortable niceties— if something was said that sounded perfunctory, he looked right at you. It wasn't a pleasant look. It was searching and confrontational at the same time. It was hard to find a way to be there and have it matter.

The second time I went was the same. I had said my goodbyes, trying to be a little casual while knowing it might be the last time. I left and then went back to his room. He was looking away as I explained that I had left something, picked it up, and said goodbye again. His head was still turned away. I stopped in the doorway and said, "John." He finally looked up at me, right into my eyes, and with my heart, I said, "I love you." He kept looking into my eyes—his eyes got warm and sad as he said, "I love you too." We both had tears.

Larry Ross

I met John through a television show called *Center Stage* sponsored by Charles Bussey, the first African American mayor in Little Rock (1970). Later I came to know that John had kinfolks who lived in my neighborhood. Charles Bussey was well before his time making talent shows available for young people to participate. I recall John participated in one of those shows with another saxophonist by the name of David I. From there, John would sit in on gigs with Henry Shead and Art Porter.

John entered AM& N College in Pine Bluff, and I to Philander Smith College in Little Rock. We would play together for jam sessions in the city. Our relationship started there. We began to play together consistently when he formed The New Directions Band.

The New Directions enjoined me—they came to me and asked me to be their drummer. At the time, I was busy with family, career, and playing six nights a week with Henry Shead, another well-known musician from Arkansas. When Henry moved to Las Vegas, I decided to stay in Little Rock and take another path in my career. I became a business executive and later a presiding elder with the Methodist Church.

I will never forget our opportunity to participate in the National Collegiate Jazz Festival sponsored by the University of Indiana. The New Directions, our band, won the competition and took a European tour. The president of AM&N College, Dr. Lawrence A.

206

Davis (known as Prexy), was the innovator in getting our group involved in this competition through the University of Indiana. This was definitely an "out of the box" opportunity. Prior to leaving for Europe, we spent two or three days in New York City. While on tour, we sailed from port to port in Europe, and we had the opportunity to play with Dave Brubeck and other musicians.

There were five of us in the group. I was the youngest member. The other four members—Sonelius Smith, Ben Jones, James Leary, and John—were the writers in the group. I recall the writing and arranging of the song "Midnight Over Memphis." Having four writers in the group really made our music unique.

While on the European tour, we were on a cruise ship playing at various venues and different ports. Many major musicians, those way ahead of the curve, were on this cruise ship. I recall John and I sitting up all night talking about the world, life in general, landing on the moon, etc. Everyone was sleep, but John and I solved the world's challenges. We did not fall asleep until the sun rose in the morning.

I would like the world to remember that John Stubblefield was a grand musician. He played well, wrote well, and was a friend— these types of things make a relationship better. John could play with whomever and was well-respected by his fellow musicians.

Lauren Sevian

I started playing with the Mingus Big Band in 2003 and was fortunate to sit next to John. At that time, I was 23 or 24, and I was definitely nervous about what I was walking into. While sitting next to John, I found that he was super cool. He was like an older brother. He would help me out with the music. It was a very special time for me.

My first impression of John was he was larger than life and fun to be around. He really inspired me and taught me a lot about "the music." I was very lucky to be able to play in the section with him. There was this power he presented in his playing. He had such a sound that was immediately identifiable. My musical impression is that he exuded this genuine power and presence. I remember his charts were all handwritten, something you seldom saw, but this was a huge part of his personality and his knowledge of "the music." Also, he was instrumental in connecting people. As I look back, it was John who introduced me to the artist Werner Meyer in Switzerland, a connection I had not expected. If you ever question why you were in the music business, this reality reaffirms to me what I felt then and now as my purpose: music.

I had so much respect for John. As a young musician starting out, to be in the Mingus Big Band and sit next to John Stubblefield—pinch me…

I recall my first road trip with the band. We went to Israel, Switzerland, and Italy. While at the airport, I became really sick to my stomach. John immediately began to seek out help for me. He told me he was going to find a doctor or nurse. He did find someone and told them I needed some medication, I was ill. I had only known John for a few months, and there he was, treating me as if I were his sister. He totally took over knowing I was ill. Personally, I did not know what to do. He made sure I was going to be taken care of. When we got on the plane, he continued to see that I was taken care of by asking the attendants to bring ginger ale, tea, etc. I told him I really appreciated his looking out for me in this way. This occurred in 2003.

Again, this was my first experience with the band on the road. This warmed my heart. It was nice to be in a band and have someone I really felt connected to. John and Frank Lacy would carry my suitcase for me. They treated me like a lady. John was always so respectful, sweet, funny, and a joy to be around. I was not on the April 2004 tour when John became ill. I was told he had to be placed in a wheel chair to be transported from the airport. He was really ill.

On another occasion, I remember we had these hotel rooms in Switzerland and we were all opening our windows and waving at each other from the windows. Just lots of fun, acting goofy and enjoying ourselves. Once, we all got some small dolphins that made noise, and we were all squeezing them like kids. I can truly bear witness to the fun side of John.

I did visit John while he was in Calvary Hospital. I usually went with Sue at the point he was upright in the bed. We would be there hanging out with him. The last time I saw him was before he passed away. It was tough to see that side of him. He was heavily medicated. That day, I was at the hospital with Craig, Abraham, and Sue. I am really glad I was able to see him before his transition. John knew we were there. I know this because he was able to acknowledge us. I will never forget that driving back from that visit, we made a wrong turn and were headed to Queens rather than Manhattan. We tried to persuade the attendant to let us turn around without paying an additional toll. I recall Sue saying, "Sir, please let us through," but the attendant said sorry but we had to pay.

One final thing I will always remember. John was arranging the music for "Song of Orange." When he finished the song, he asked me if I wanted my part. Not long after that I received a letter from John that contained my part. Who else would share the music with me before time other than John, giving me a head start in practicing my parts.

I really would like people to remember his heart. John had a heart larger than life. He had a kindness about him that a lot of people do not have. He did not have to look out for me, but that was who he was. He had a love for the people around him. He was beautiful both inside and out. There needs to be more people in the world like John. I always felt this way about him. I had a lot of love and tremendous respect for him. His spirit is with us. He was there gently walking me through my formative years in the band.

Alex Sipiagin

I have been playing with the Mingus Big Band since 1995 and had the biggest privilege to work with John Stubblefield for several years. He was always incredibly encouraging and supportive. Because of him, I gained a lot of confidence. He always commented and was always positive about my solos. His music and performance were always on the super-highest level. From what I remember, each time he took a solo, he put himself 100% into it no matter what we played, whether at a huge jazz festival or tiny jazz club.

He had the ability to put everyone in the band and the audience in a certain mood, the special "Stubbs" mood, almost like a meditational and serene mood. If there were any disagreements in the band (and believe me, there were some), John was always the mediator and cooling everybody down. If somebody in the band did not have a chance to play solo in the set, John was the one who made sure they got their turn. His humor was always right on time, and your mood would change right away when he said something.

One little short story comes straightaway to my head. I remember we were flying to Japan with the Mingus Big Band back in 1999. I had fallen asleep in my seat, and someone woke me up. I opened my eyes, and it was John standing right next to me with McCoy Tyner. He said, "Alex, I am sorry to wake you up, but I just want to introduce a great friend of mine, and most amazing musician, McCoy Tyner." (McCoy was traveling on the same flight to the same festival to perform with Michael Brecker.) I couldn't believe it. It was like I was still dreaming. The way John introduced me to McCoy, it was so special to me. He said so many nice things about me right there to McCoy Tyner. I couldn't fall asleep for the rest of the flight, as I was so moved by this gesture from John.

Last time I had a chance to see John was I think around 2004 or 2005. It was probably his last tour with the Mingus Band. We ended up sitting on the plane together on the way from Europe. He never told anybody about his disease, and even more, he never showed anybody he was in pain. He always looked the same: spiritual and peaceful. I remember I ordered a drink from the flight attendant, and I asked John what he wanted to drink. He said, "Give me exactly what you ordered." I said "John this is a triple vodka. Are you sure?" His reply was, "Yes, absolutely." It was our last cheers together.

Steve Slagle

I met John in New York City in the early 80s. He had been in NYC for a while, I do not recall the exact time. I was new in town and would go to hear bands play throughout the city. John was the kind of guy who knew who was new in town. When I did meet him, he already knew me. We became close when we were in the Mingus Big Band in the 90s. John was the voice of the tenor. When I would write an arrangement, I would not write for an instrument but for the person. That person was John. That is how close we became. He was always very encouraging to me. When I started writing for the band, he was extremely encouraging. He lived in the East Village and I lived in Brooklyn. We were on the road all the time and traveled all over the world together.

To me John definitely reached back to the vaudeville days of entertainment. It seemed as if John innately had DNA that reached back to that time, a time when jazz was evolving. In vaudeville, a musician would be able to work. I feel like John had a connection with that. If John had not been a sax player, he could have been a vaudeville comedian. He improvised. He could be very funny, a great MC; he could take a mike and be an incredible MC of the show, making jokes that made people feel good. This was a talent John had that other people might not have known.

Once when we were in Nice France, the piano player in the bar was playing real square. There were musicians from all over the world attending the Nice Jazz Festival, and here we were listening to someone who did not play very well. John discretely went up to him and asked what time he would be finished and if John could MC a show for the musicians in the bar. The piano player finished around midnight, and John took it from there. He did his thing from midnight until 4:00 a.m. He brought musicians on stage, told jokes. Everyone had a great time. He even went into a comedy routine like Richard Pryor, Robin Williams—yes, that level of greatness. It was impromptu, and it was a great experience to see John in that posture. It was a great night. He could improvise and make the world a better place.

John was a *Gentleman*. He treated people in a very dignified way. He had a certain politeness in his way of meeting and introducing people. He would say, "I want you to meet one of my worthy colleagues, Steve Slagle." This was consistent. He was always like that. A little like a politician (not a phony one, but a real politician, a person who wants people to have a healthy community) and a little bit Southern. Being in NYC, we do not get a lot of the Southern influence. I am from Southern California, which is more southern, so I appreciated his Southern influence. He did not have a Southern accent. His accent if anything was NYC. It was just the way he conducted himself.

I always thought John was a very high-level musician. I heard him before I met him and recognized he was a great player. In the late 90s, the one thing I tried to do was encourage him to record more in his own name. His response was that people were not offering him the right money. There is a line between art and business. If you are offered a great contract, good, but you have to paint the picture of the goal you want. I tried to encourage him by saying that sometimes you have to do it anyway. If he had stayed healthy, he would have recorded more on his own.

I saw him at the highest point of his life in the 90s when he had three or four of the best gigs in the city—Mingus Big Band, Fort Apache Band, McCoy Tyner. He was doing four jobs at once and very much in demand. He was at the top of his thing here in New York. This did not change him. He was not egocentric.

I think about John all the time, the laughter he had and the good times, his way of communicating and being with people. When we toured, we all had our individual hotel rooms. He would open the door of his room, and you could see him in bed writing post cards—he always sent post cards. There would be musicians in the room laughing and joking. To John, this was life at its best.

I also remember he was so affected by Princess Diana's death he started crying. That was a surprise to me. I had no idea he had a soft place in his heart about her. He was really affected by that. He and I were at a bar around 11:00 p.m. in Chicago when we heard it.

A remarkable thing about John was his sense of community— like a preacher in a small town, one who had a big following and was community-minded. Someone to go to get some empathy and solace. Not everyone is like that. His congregation was anyone who was part of his community. He was very sensitive and always ready to reach out to them and help them through a problem or give advice, have dinner. That is one thing I sorely miss. In the last decade the sense of community has been shattered. We need more people more like John. What he did went beyond music. He was a little bit political in a good way.

President Bill Clinton visited him in the hospital, and I find some similarities in that the idea of community made them similar. John would call people "governor." When I first heard that, it felt like something I had read in a text book. He called me "the general" out of a sense of respect, being the band leader. I really miss John. No words I could say could adequately communicate the loss of this special person.

Charles Smith

My earliest memory of John was during the mid-50s. I met him through another friend in the neighborhood, Otis Strickland, who lived a few doors down from me on Izard Street. Otis's cousin Wendell Jones lived a few blocks over on Chester Street, and John and Wendell were next-door neighbors. As children, we played together on many occasions, but we attended different elementary schools. My mom was a teacher at Carver Elementary, and this is where I attended. John, Otis, and Wendell attended Booker T. Washington Elementary School. We remained close and spent many hours together playing in the neighborhood. In seventh grade, we all entered Dunbar Junior High School where we played together in the band.

In junior high, we began our music experience learning to play the flute-a-phone. John selected his instrument of choice, the tenor saxophone, while Wendell and I chose clarinet. John was dedicated to music from the beginning. He loved it! I used to watch him carry that big tenor saxophone case. The interior was of plywood, heavy. I remember him lugging that big case to and from school each day. He did not care; music truly became a big part of his life. John quite frankly was a brilliant musician. I always thought of him as Coltrane. The sound he produced was mellow and very avant-garde. He could play all genres of music and was good in that respect. He sent me an album when I lived in Dallas entitled *Sophisticated Lady*. One of the songs on that album was "Midnight Over Memphis." This was and remains my favorite. I do not know why I have held onto this song all these years, but I have.

As kids, I remember we spent a lot of time racing our wagons and go-carts down the hill on Izard Street. I would race in my red wagon, and John, his brother William, Otis, his brother Tyrone, and Wendell, and I would show up for the race. We had hours of fun seeing who could win. After the race was over, it was back to the drawing board to repair the carts for more races. I recall one day I was riding my wagon backwards and it flipped and I scrapped my knuckles—to this day I still carry those battle scars. Things we did as kids, what fun. On another occasion I recall a specific basketball game. Another friend of ours, Roddy Collins, and I were both the same size, a bit shorter than John and Otis, but we were quick and fast and took them on for a game of doubles. Roddy and I beat them that day, and John and I laughed about that game for years.

Although John was a year older than I was, we remained close friends throughout our high school and college years. During those years, the military draft was in full blast, and we were the only two in our neighborhood who were in college. The rest of the guys were in the military. While at the University of Arkansas at Fayetteville, I saw a flyer where people were going to Illinois to work at a packing plant. I saw this as a way to earn money during the summer. I talked to John about it, and we decided to apply. This is one experience John and I never ever forgot! We wondered if we could get on, yeah! They needed people. We were hired immediately and paid $2.35 per hour. Both John and I had relatives in Chicago, and we got money from our parents, packed up, caught the train, and headed that way.

After a short visit with relatives, we headed for Rochelle where we were greeted to a large dormitory full of bunk beds. My assigned bed was on the bottom bunk below a 300-pound guy. This was a rude awakening among a menagerie of people. John and I were more than fascinated with another guy who worked with us and loved ice cream. The interesting thing about this man was that he would bring ice cream from the cafeteria in his pocket wrapped in a napkin. Of course, it was melted before he arrived at the dormitory, but he did this the whole time we were there. John and I worked in different departments, and his assignment was more physically stressful than mine. He finally had enough and left before me and returned to Chicago. This was truly an eye-opening experience for the two of us.

One last experience most people might not know about John is that while he was in college, one of his music instructors, Brooks, served as a talent scout for students and would get jobs in Mississippi and throughout the South during the summer for students to work with groups traveling the circuit. John shared with me that one of his jobs was playing in Ike and Tina Turner's band in Mississippi. He told me he was in the bandstand playing, and Tina was dancing and he began to focus on Tina. He was jamming and looking at Tina shake her butt. He was observed doing this and was fired from the gig. As a result of this, he was stranded in Mississippi and had to phone his dad to send money for his transportation home. He told me he had a conversation with his dad regarding this situation, and his dad asked, "Are you really serious about this being your life's work?" When John said he was, his dad replied, "Okay."

We returned to school and completed our degrees. Eventually we both found ourselves in Chicago again during the time the draft was in full force, but neither of us knew the other was there, too. I had received my "Dear John letter" of notification for the draft. While walking near the Illinois Central Commuter Station on Stoney Island Avenue, he saw me and called to me from the platform. This was really a chance happening, meeting John at the station. We exchanged information and stayed in touch. Like everyone at that time, we were concerned about being drafted, especially me, inasmuch as I had received letters from the draft board. So, John and I got together and went to the University of Chicago to receive counseling services for those looking for strategies to stay out of Vietnam. Ironically, during the discussion with the counselor, John revealed he had not received any information from the draft board. The counselor advised him if no one had sent him any paperwork, it must be lost. If John had not been contacted, he should let things be as they were. I received my deferment, and both John and I became teachers in the Chicago school district.

We were slowly but surely maturing as we made our way in our new world. I remember one very, very cold Chicago night, he called me to tell me someone had broken into his apartment and stolen his instruments. Not good, his instruments! I helped him move to another apartment in Hyde Park. Then he met and married Sharon Seaberry, a kindergarten teacher he met while serving as an itinerant music teacher in the Chicago school district. Not long after that came the bad news: John announced he and Sharon were moving to New York City, but we still continued to keep in touch and visit through the years,

I want everyone to remember that John was an excellent musician with a warm smile. He was a loving and kind man, a lot of fun to be with, a guy's guy. His smile was infectious and was always with him. I will always remember his birthday party in February 2005 where you could see and feel the love and affection of the many musicians in attendance. I recall assisting John when leaving the party. He was happy and smiling. During one visit, I remember Wendell was standing behind John, and John was smiling in spite of his lingering pain. Wendell was beginning to tear up and we both knew John was really sick. But there John was in the fight for his life, smiling—he was able to deal with it. That was an important moment for me; his warmth near the end of his life was still present. John was a true friend, and I am thankful to have been a part of his life. I have several computers in my home, and every day each of them starts with John's picture.

Sonelius Smith

I met John while attending AM&N College, now the University of Arkansas at Pine Bluff (UAPB). One day while walking on campus, I ran into John, and he asked me if I had heard about the new music group on campus, and I said no. He then said, "Yes, there is a new group, and we need a piano player and you are that piano player." I said, "Well okay." We already had a music relationship prior to this meeting in that I had the Sonelius Smith Band and John had joined me in my band earlier. I recall we were paid $17 per night for our performances.

My first impression of John was that he was very enthusiastic—unrelenting enthusiasm. We were searching to expand our knowledge and techniques in the music, and that all came to us with the progression of time.

My thoughts regarding John, myself, and all musicians is that we are all average; however, with the right opportunities we can all become genius. John could compete with any musician out there. He played on the highest of levels with people. John could compete with any musician on the planet.

Most of my experiences with John were in college and the European Tour that the New Directions Band won in the late 60s. During the tour in Europe, members of the band met Dave Brubeck. He was a really nice guy. They called him "The Saint" because he never had anything bad to say about anyone. I saw Dave Brubeck preform a few days before his transition. We were all young musicians at the time, and we were glad to meet a musician of his stature.

I also recall going to Chicago and spending time with John at his in-laws' home. That day we had dinner, and John and I played music all afternoon as they sat on the sofa and listened to us.

I want the world to remember John was a good man.

John and I met through a mutual friend, Bill Cody. Bill was a well-known musician in New York and also a narcotics agent. He and John played at the Village Vanguard. Bill introduced John to me and told me John played the saxophone and oboe. John sort of brushed off the fact he played oboe—and I too thought "oboe." A few weeks later, I was at Bill's for a lesson, and John came by. John played the oboe that day, and he did it very well. Bill used to talk to me about a lot of musicians.

In 1979, John and I played in Sam Rivers' band, and I sat next to him. Rivers' band had a big horn section with 10 saxophones (three altos, two tenors, two baritones, three sopranos). John played both soprano sax and oboe.

In 2003, John and I played with Abdullah Ibrahim's band. Abdullah was from Cape Town, South Africa, and was known for his temperament as a bandleader. I recall the story that Abdullah upset John enough for John to pull a knife on him. Abdullah was verbally aggressive to musicians and everyone knew this. At this particular time, he made John mad, and John told me later he had never been that mad before.

All of this happened while on tour in South Africa. We were there 10 days traveling to various places. It was during this time I got to know John really well. John left the band upon our return to the states, but he recommended Wayne Escoffrey as his replacement. I understand John left the band because he could not make some of the upcoming engagements.

My first impression of John was that he was a cool, reserved guy. He was very calm and talked about things in a manner as if he were a teacher. He talked a lot about saxophones. He had an interest in the different models that were out at that time, and he talked about music today versus music of the past. He was kind of put off by the profane language that was coming about in the music. He was not too cool with that. He was easy to talk to, and if you needed advice from him, he gave it freely. He never talked bad about anybody. If someone was not on a certain music level, he would just raise his eyebrows like Mr. Spock in *Star Trek*. John's style of playing was compared to that of Wayne Shorter who worked years earlier with Art Blakely and Miles Davis. We, along with Bill Cody, often told John his music was changing and very reminiscent of that of Wayne Shorter. John took it as a compliment when Bill would call him the new Wayne Shorter.

I recall while we were on tour in South Africa, John met a diplomat from that country. She held a very high office in South Africa, but I do not recall her name. John met her and they got along pretty well. Every night we performed; she was there. Two weeks after we returned to NYC, I got a call from her looking for John. To my surprise, he had given her my number and not his. I had to argue with her for several minutes to get her off the phone. I told her John had given her the wrong number. She was calling because she was coming to NYC for a meeting at the United Nations and wanted to see John. When I told him about this, he just laughed. I said to him, "John you are married right?" and he said he was. I said, "I see that is why you gave her my number to throw her off your trail." I do not know if she ever got in touch with him. Being a diplomat, she probably had access to a lot of information, but I never found out if she was able to contact him. John left the band after that tour.

The tour to South Africa was our only trip together. We spent time talking about horns, music. The personnel in the band were not stable, and musicians would come and go each time we had a road gig. I was surprised Abdullah had called John back to the band. During a dinner before the first performance in South Africa, Abdullah sat next to John and put his arm around his shoulder and said, "All is forgiven." This was a sign that things were okay between them. We were glad to see this happen. We all knew that Abdullah was one to push one to the brink. Abdullah corroborated the story that he did the wrong thing to bring John to this type emotion. It was good that Abdullah was willing to make up, and he really wanted John to stay longer, but John had other obligations. John was prominently featured while on the tour in South Africa. Ironically, both John and Abdullah had prostate cancer at the same time. Abdullah now lives in Germany.

I recall we were rehearsing with Abdullah's band, and the drummer could not follow directions. John nudged me and said, "Abdullah is going to get up and get on the drums." No sooner than John said that, Abdullah walked over to the drummer and played what he wanted to hear. John then said, "Take a good look at the drummer because he will not be around much longer." Sure, enough the drummer did not return.

I would like the world to know that John was the kind of person who was very forthcoming in passing on what he knew about music. He was not selfish. He wanted the younger musicians to know what he knew and not to have to go through what he had to make it.

Albert Sun

My first actual interaction with John was on a flight to Italy in October 1999. This was my first tour with the band, and we were headed to Milan. While boarding, John was having problems trying to store his instruments in the overhead bin on the plane. You see, John never let anyone take his instruments. They always stayed near him. Things were getting a little heated between John and the flight attendant, so I put my hand up trying to mediate the situation, and I apparently put my hand up too close to John's face. His response was, "Mr. Sun, so this is a talk-to-the-hand moment"!

My impression of John is that he was one of the senior members of the band, and I always respected him for that. He was an old school entertainer who had a lot of talent, but first and foremost he was a performer. People paid good money to see a show, and John always felt we had to give them their money's worth. As a musician, I loved John. He was incredible, and I liked that he sacrificed a lot of his abilities for the band. John would do the blues solos; he had no problems being a team player.

These are just a few of my experiences with John. There were many. Before going on stage, John used to say, "Men, there's red meat out there. Let's go out there and be somebody!" This would loosen up the band and prepare for the night.

Sound Check

I recall one thing I did not look forward to was sound check because we had the most difficult sound-check process. Everyone was supposed to check their mic and monitor levels, but our band never had a traditional sound check. They would rehearse during that time, and fine tuning the levels often didn't happen until the first song. This led to some tempestuous times, often following an overnight flight or long travel episode. I do know that when we had a really tough sound check, the show was good. If sound check was too smooth, we got worried. There was no other experience like it. We had so many virtuosos, and we had to balance everyone's individual talents within the context of a 90-minute set. Sue [Mingus] always insisted the main focal point be Charles' music, but it was the individual personalities that made the band what it was about, and that was the hard part, having no real leader. We had an appointed band leader, but it was the elder members who always kept the balance.

Clermont-Ferrand

Many of our tours were difficult because of the scheduling. We would fly into a city, play that night, and leave for the next city early the next morning. We all had incidents where we hung out at the bar a little longer than we should have. But this one night in Clermont-Ferrand, we had a 6:00 a.m. leave for a bus ride to Lyon and two flights to Sweden. I got up to load the equipment on the bus at 5:00 a.m., and I noticed John Hicks and Stubbs still sipping cognac in the bar. I suggested they both start to get packed and ready for a 6:00 a.m. departure. By 6:00 a.m. only Hicks had made it down, so I went to get John and found him passed out in his room with clothes in his hand. A couple of bandmates helped me get him and his bags to the bus so we could get underway. At some point Stubbs got his second wind and began walking up and down the aisle preaching to us about how it was in Moms Mabley's organization—they would leave no one behind. He was still buzzed and went up and down the aisles entertaining us all until we arrived at the airport. It was a long morning. By the time we got to our next gig, he found out someone had recorded his rant. This was a memorable experience we used to kid John about all the time.

UC Davis

Another memory that sticks out is when we performed at UC Davis in CA. As usual the band would always decide what they were going to play right before the set. The band members were meeting over dinner, and of course the question came up "What should we play?" I said, "Man, I would like to hear Cumbia."

John came up to me and said, "Mr. Sun, we got the music," and he closed the door to the dressing room. From then on, every time I've tried to make a recommendation or suggestion, I was reminded by someone with John's famous quote, "We got the music, Mr. Sun."

Steamed

This is the "Shower Story." While on the road, John would use steam to get the wrinkles out of his clothes before performing. I went to drop off something at his room, and he answered the door in his boxers, nylon socks, skullcap—it was a funny sight. I asked him what he was doing. The whole room was full of steam. He told me he turns on the hot shower for steam and this gets the wrinkles out of his clothes. John was always dressed to the 9s.

Battle in Aarhus

Once we were in Denmark and we were doing a show in a venue that did not have a back stage, only a curtain partition that separated us from the audience. It had been a rough travel day and tempers were short. Earl McIntyre had already gone off on me for suggesting that if he wanted more room on the bus to put his horn in the trailer. One of the discussions ensued about what tunes would be played that night. It was Stubbs and Philip Harper's turn to get into it. It got real verbal over whether "Jump Monk" or "Moanin'" should be played. Little did we know a reporter was within ear shot of the yelling and wrote a review regarding the band in his paper the next morning. Knowing the temperament of Charles Mingus, the reporter wrote in his review, "The band listened to a tape of Charles Mingus scolding the band to get warmed up before performing one of the best shows I've heard," when in fact what he heard was a disagreement among band members that night.

Touch of Class

John was the consummate entertainer. He would always make eye contact with someone in the crowd and acknowledge their presence. He always believed that you had to connect with your audience. Give it your all and make it count. Make them remember how special it was. Give them respect. He was always polite and gracious!

Sad Moment

Finally, as I stated earlier, John always kept his instruments close to him when he traveled. At the end of his last tour in April 2004, he checked in his horn. I had never seen him give his horn as checked bags to travel underneath the airplane—that was something he had NEVER done. It broke my heart when I saw that.

Remembering

I would like the world to know that when John left the band, it was a huge loss, one that we've never really recovered from. He was the heart and soul of the band, and we never realized how important a role he played. There is a void there—no one to set an example. John brought balance and class to the band. The Mingus band was unique in that there was no Charles Mingus to set the rules. On the road we had to rely on the senior members to take a stand when things got out of hand. Someone to put their foot down in a particular situation. You know, like when brothers fight and the parents put their foot down to stop the confusion. I will always remember John had those "old school" values. We learned a lot from John. We really did not notice it until he was gone. Yes, the band was much more passionate when John was there.

Henry Threadgill

I first met John in Chicago sometime between the end of 1968 and April of 1969. We were members of the Association for the Advancement of Creative Musicians (AACM). At that time, we lived close to each other. John was on 51st and Drexel on Hyde Park Boulevard, and I lived on 49th. around the corner from Jessie Jackson's Bread Basket. Another musician, Douglas Ewart, stayed across the street from John. We were all involved with the AACM and became good friends. Our families were close, we shared dinners together, and our children were born about the same time. The three of us were always in touch.

John was a very talented musician, a powerhouse and an original person. He was very interesting. He had a strong foot in traditional music such as avant-garde. The AACM embraced experiential and avant-garde music, and that is how we were classified.

John was well respected and an extremely talented instrumentalist. He came to New York City and got in the fray; he had the talent to compete. Like in the world of boxing, John came up quick. When he was in the ring, John won. We all knew what was going on in his career.

John was a class A musician who gave 150%. He was not the type to play just because it was a gig. He did not do "just passing," because that lacks a lot. He put his spirit into his music and went beyond the evident of physicality. He demonstrated his talent with many bands, which include Charles Mingus, Kenny Barron, Thad Jones, McCoy Tyner, Fort Apache, Quiet Fire, and my band the Society Situation Dance Band and others. We played in Europe more than in the United States, and John was always there. He was not a tactician; as stated before, he did not give you something just to pass. He had spirit in what he gave. This is why so many people wanted him in their band, they loved him. All I know is that John was one of the most serious players out there.

We played a lot of music together!

John and I played all types of music together—blues, rock, jazz, etc. He played in Society Situation Dance Band from the beginning. We had lots of fun. The audience went wild over us in Europe. I especially remember John's performance in Hamburg, Germany, which can be viewed anytime on YouTube.

John and I used to have a contest to see who could write the most music every week. I would beat him every time. He would write some good music, but he could not keep up with me. We did

this because it was a way to keep our creative imagination stimu-
lated. We would also play the music we wrote, and this kept us
motivated through this exchange of music.

John and his wife Sharon were the first to leave Chicago and
move to New York. This was a big move. When I left Chicago and
moved to the city, I stayed with them. I recall someone broke into
their apartment while I was there. At that time, people would tie
things around their waist and lower themselves into your house
and take all they could carry.

I recall while in Chicago John and I were in the Phil Cohran
Orchestra. We got fired, both of us! Phil said we were fine musicians but we could not do as we were told. He wanted us to improvise with a limited amount of material. We thought it was square.
After all, we were young cats in the band, and we thought we knew
more than he. Eventually, we found out he knew more as we continued to progress in our knowledge of the music. Again, he told
us he was letting us go because we could not do as we were told.
You see, Phil viewed music from an Egyptologist mode, and he
wanted John and me to play in that way. Finally, there came a split
between the philosophical approach and the nationalistic approach.
With the split, a part of the group went west with Phil, who
embraced nationalism, and the other went east with Muhal
Abrams. The group that arrived on the east coast did not wish to
be pigeon holed. They just wanted to play music for all people. This
is the group John and I followed with the desire to play original
music. Phil was brilliant—he did us a favor by firing us.

Before leaving Chicago, I recall John had an opportunity to play
with what is now known as the Earth, Wind, and Fire Band. When
asked to join, he declined, and I understand he made that decision
on the fact he was not meant to do that. That music was too commercial. To say yes to that type of music would have been a sell out
for John. He had big ideas, and to take their job offer would have
been selling out to something he did not have in his spirit to do.

John's dream was to follow the road of the masters—Duke Ellington, Charlie Parker, John Coltrane, Count Basie, etc. They were originals, and that is what he wanted to study and perfect.

John was a very kind and giving person. He was generous with time as much as he was a fantastic artist. There is something about giving to people on that level. John was on the highest level.

Jack Walrath

I cannot recall when and where I first met John, but in the 80s I recall he did a rehearsal with my band (Masters of Suspense) and we played together with the Mingus Big Band.

John was always very gracious, very nice, and a great musician. He and I played with Mingus in the early days. We were very aware of Mingus' concept of music. John would bring in charts for the big band. His charts were the only arrangements that captured the Mingus concept. John played with Mingus, and he captured that Mingus concept. This again was easy for John because he understood Mingus and his approach to music.

John was a great musician. The first time he came in and played with my band, he nailed it right away. He was great. When I think of John, I just know that he and I were around Mingus, we studied him, and we were able to continue writing charts that followed the Mingus concept. Things have changed now, and that approach to music is no longer embraced. However, while alive, John continued to write the charts and play the music with great poise and improvisation.

I wrote the chart for a piece called "Hogg Callin' Blues." John was featured on this piece, and he played it from his heart and soul. When he played this tune, it would bring people out of their seats. It was a showpiece for him, and he perfected it. We would have crowds of people standing around giving a standing ovation when he finished his solo. This piece we played again and again, but I will never forget the first time it took us to another place.

I remember I met John on the street one time, and he gave me a video of the Mingus Big Band. When I watched it, it blew me away. I am glad he gave it to me. It is a constant reminder of how the band sounded back then. I still have it, and I treasure it because John gave it to me and that was the last time we were together.

I recall John and I had a conversation one time outside the Thyme café. He asked me how old, and I was I told him I was 57. He told me I had to watch out for my health. He told me I had to keep up with my health. It was a heartfelt conversation that I will never forget. He talked very seriously. Perhaps he was ill at that time, but he did not discuss that. He only talked about me taking care of my health. We had this discussion about two years before he died.

He was a great musician, had no attitude, and was always trying to move forward. John was one of the good guys always encouraging! That was rare back when we first met and is rare now.

York Wilburn, Sr.

[Provided by his son York Wilburn, Jr.]

My dad always spoke about greatness, very loving, when he would mention John as a band member. He stated that John had the ability to improvise. When traveling as a band, he could adapt to any audience. He also talked often about how excited John was when he recorded his first album with York Wilburn and the Thrillers.

My dad also mentioned how proud John was when their band ended desegregation at the "Top of the Rock Club" in the Tower Building in Little Rock. The Tower Building was the brainchild of Former Governor Winthrop Rockefeller.

In conclusion, my dad demanded professionalism in music, behavior. He also demanded dressing with integrity. He stated that John never disappointed him. He always displayed amazing professionalism in all areas.

And he was very kind and loving toward all.

Booker T. Williams

John found his *"raison d'etre."* He was not just to play music but specifically, the saxophone. He and I first met while walking down the street in the Village. We were aware of each other, but had not really met. On that day, we just bumped into each other and exchanged greetings—how are things going, who are you playing with. The conversation was very brief and fast moving. In New York, you always run into musicians on the way to and from rehearsals. Subsequently, we would run into each other from time to time.

I looked up to him as a brother and mentor, not necessarily verbalized but through osmosis, e.g., body language, nonverbal communication. Just being around him for a period of time things started to rub off.

John was very serious about "the music." There are many pitfalls in the life of a musician, but John was focused and did not let those things deter him. When mentoring, he did not always break things down in simple terms. It was more you are here with me, you are on you own, I am demonstrating things to you, and this is how you learn. John taught by example.

We became musically connected when we went to Europe with Threadgill. This is when I first played with John and we really got to know each other. We talked about our horns, mouthpieces, reeds, etc. John would make recommendations on what I might try. From that point, we did a lot of rehearsing together, and I really got to know a lot more about him. We shared things with each other; there were no feelings of threat. The greater part of our communication was nonverbal. Much of what John would do, I would watch him and learn. He was not the type who did not want to share with others. He and I sat side by side as we played tenor in the horn section of the band. John also played soprano.

The music was both improvisational and magical in that the music we played allowed us to deviate from the charts. While there were sections where we had to play the music as written, many times the music was moving so fast, we had to break down the complicated lines as the only two saxophone players and make it happen. We had creativity and flexibility to make it work through the chemistry and from the craftsmanship of the art. Our concerts were not cookie cutter; we played avant-garde and were ready to create. There would be sections where John would grab the direction, I would listen and follow him, and again there was a chemistry to make this happen. If the chemistry had not been there, this would have been difficult. It brought out what was in our spirit and our heart. John and I worked very well together.

As the band leader, Threadgill knew what he wanted and he selected John and me to play in the horn section. The band members were selected based on Threadgill's knowledge of the talent he wanted and needed to bring the chemistry to the band. The music was vibrant and fresh, never sounding like a rehearsal. A lot of our success came from experience where our music became more about concept and not music. The chemistry was there and the music aspect became secondary. Threadgill brought the musicians who had the craftsmanship to pull that off. John was a craftsman.

When John and I worked together, concept and chemistry was there! It was like being at war in the trenches; we had each other's back. We leaned on each other. We were peers. Where he was weak, I was strong and vice versa. This is an example of where I picked up a lot from John through nonverbal communication. I was around him long enough where there was an exchange of chemistry. Traveling and playing with John was a great experience. After the tour, we had a higher level of knowing each other, no longer just passing on the street with a hand shake. There was laughter, high fives, chatting, and an embrace.

John was a reed specialist/perfectionist. Often, I saw him shaving his reeds in between breaks and during rehearsals. Purchasing reeds is an ongoing challenge. They do not make them the way they used to. The quality of the reed has declined since they found cheaper ways to produce them. You may buy a box of 25 of which only two are good. Rather than throw them away, I remember John perfected his reeds by shaving them down. I called the bad reeds a dud, but John would make those duds work. Reeds are affected by the weather and gravity. They can change like mood swings. Rather than throw away an imperfect reed, John perfected them to be what he needed them to be. He became in tune to the reed and to himself. John was very meticulous, fine-tuned, and laser-focused about "the music." It takes a certain type of person to do that, and that was John. He perfected his reeds in order to create his sound and his sound was his voice. When you heard John play, you knew it was him. This showed me how meticulous he was about his love for music. This reed shaving is very time-consuming, but he had the patience to make it happen because he knew the perfection of the reed brought quality to the sound of his music.

I got to know John a lot better talking with his sister, Joyce. She filled in the blanks with information that only a sister would know. I am blessed now to know those things. John was kind and giving. He was true blue.

Reggie Workman

I met John many years ago back in the late 70s in New York City. At that time, he was called for many studio engagements. He was one of the first-call players in New York. If people had a project, they would call John Stubblefield because he could handle the situation. He had a musical personality, and he worked with many of the forerunners in the music business while doing his own projects. He was incredible person, a great composer and easy to get along with.

I liked John a lot. He was a great musician, very concise in the way he approached the music. He was reluctant when I asked him to cut loose from the norm as we were looking for a new voice in the music. In most cases John liked to stick to the rules but in this case, he did deviate when I asked him to come into my group and do something different. Being a stellar musician, John could deal with all that came his way.

There was a time when Howard Johnson and John would get together and do experimental things with instruments and the score. When John could not make an engagement and I had to find a replacement for him, he would sometimes come around to listen to the musician who took his place. Once he came to listen to a young aspiring multi-instrumentalist, Arthur Rhames. John's only comment was "Wow." That was one of his favorite expressions.

John developed a style of his own, which was phenomenal as he had come out of Chicago where he was surrounded by so many powerful musicians. Unfortunately, John made his transition before he was able to do all the things he wanted to do.

Appendix

Explanations of Songs

Over the years, John cataloged his body of work by listing his discography and his recorded compositions. This section of the book is dedicated to John's friend Olivier Gatto. No regrets, Olivier, for not having the opportunity to speak with John before his transition. Gaining the strength to listen to his music again, those long telephone conversations the two of you enjoyed, the time you shared together, and the music you played lives on.

In this body of work catalogued by John through the years, he continues to share his thoughts and insights into his music by describing why he wrote each composition, who it was written for, and the spirit in which it is be played. The following notes were found in his personal papers. I hope you enjoy reading John's thoughts.

I did.

King of Harts

In 1992, Billy Hart's management asked me to record with him and compose a piece for the session. I had about one week to write a song. I went back and listened to some of Billy Hart's recordings with the Herbie Hancock Sextet and Wes Montgomery. I then proceeded to write something based on his style of playing vamps and double-time rhythms. A few days before the recording, the title came to me, "King of Harts." It's my musical tribute to a great drummer.

I started writing from a vamp, and things just flowed. The piece has a 36-bar structure. I wrote the melody so that the drums would complement the melody. The song stays on two chords for maybe 16 bars, then the melody goes up a fourth, but it doesn't remain on a subdominant. It descends in minor chords. As it descends, it gives a feeling like it's turning around and the song is going back to the top.

"King of Harts" features the drums throughout the piece, playing in a double-time feeling over the pulse, complementing the melody in a timbale style. The melody was originally orchestrated for violin, guitar, and saxophone.

In interpreting this song, there should be an interplay between the melody and the drums, with the bass and piano functioning underneath that, holding things together in a rhythmic way. In terms of development and improvisation, the form should be kept, of course, but the rhythm section can react to complement what's going on behind the soloist.

Artist	Album	Label/Year
John Stubblefield	Morning Song	Enja, 1993
Billy Hart	Amethyst	Arabesque, 1992

Dialogues in Blue

"Dialogues in Blue" was written about two days before Christmas 1991. I composed it for my sister, working on my nephew's little Casio piano. What I love about the new musical instruments today is that they have all the different rhythmic grooves that you can play against. At that time I was really bending my ear listening to rhythm and blues and pop, so I used some of these musical devices for the piano part.

I knew I would be traveling to Japan to do the "Chasin' The Trane" tour in late January, a tour that featured an all-star septet playing the music of John Coltrane. When I was asked to arrange two of Coltrane's pieces for the septet, I decided to arrange "Dialogues in Blue" as well.

"Dialogues in Blue" is a 24-bar minor blues with the usual chord changes. The pianist plays a rhythmic pattern, the bass plays a *basso ostinato*, and the drums play a polyrhythmic swing, which gives a nice feel to jazz today. The melody is in the tenor saxophone and trumpet, with optional parts for three horns.

This piece should be played in a very spirited and lyrical manner.

Artist	Type of Recording	Place/Date
Chasin' The Trane	Television Program	Osaka, Japan/1992

Once Upon a Time

"Once Upon A Time" is a song that grew out of my desire to write something in memory of the great drummer and band leader Art Blakey. I also wanted to pay tribute to the other founders of the musical school known as the Jazz Messengers, so I threw in a little of Kenny Dorham and Horace Silver.

This piece is written in the hard bop style, but in composing it I realized that I didn't want the musical form to be the same as those used in the early periods of the Messengers. In many of my compositions, I've worked with different musical forms. "Once Upon A Time" has the structure of a minor blues, but the form is elongated to 48-18-24, with a tag of seven bars.

I utilized minor 11th chord sounds in changing the harmonies so that one could hear the minor blues with a slightly different twist. When I was working with Mary Lou Williams, I learned a lot about using blues forms and disguising them in different ways. In terms of counterpoint, I employed techniques used in jazz in the hard bop period that are still alive today. The tag is written in the style of Kenny Dorham.

This piece should be played in the hard bop tradition.

Artist	Album	Label/Year
Kenny Barron	Quickstep	Enja, 1991

Here and There

"Here and There" grew out of an attempt to restructure a melody in 8 bars. It has an 8-bar piano introduction with drums and bass. In the two 8-bar phrases that follow, the flugelhorn and saxophone play a cat and mouse melody in 3 bars, which is answered by the rhythm section and one instrument in 5 bars, with the bass playing a pedal point. In the second 8-bar phrase, however, the melody and harmonies are altered. Then there is a 12-bar bridge with a break, followed by an 8-bar release.

To interpret "Here and There," the feeling should be contemporary.

Artist	Album	Label/Year
John Stubblefield	Morning Song	Enja, 1993
Olivier Gatto	What Is This Thing Called Love	—, 1993
Kenny Barron	Quickstep	Enja, 1991

Sophisticated Funk

"Sophisticated Funk" was written during a recording session for Cheetah Records. Initially I was to record a jazz album, but we had problems with the musicians' time schedules and commitments. One day Teruo Nakamura, the bassist and founder of Cheetah Records, suggested we do an instrumental pop record. I didn't have material for that kind of project, so most of the music was composed on the spot.

"Sophisticated Funk" came out of my love for rhythm and blues and the music of James Brown. The song has a funky groove for 16 bars, then the harmonies descend, followed by a rhythmic release. The solos are played over a 24-bar format. The melody is written to sound as if a person were singing over the harmonic background.

"Sophisticated Funk" is an homage to blues and rhythm and all of those who like to "get on the good foot."

Artist	Album	Label/Year
John Stubblefield	Sophisticated Funk	Cheetah, 1990

Something for Ramon

"Something for Ramon" grew out of a Latin groove I wrote for Ramon Burke, one of my saxophone students at Rutgers University. When Kenny Barron recorded his album, "Live at Fat Tuesday's," he asked the band members to write something for the date, and I submitted two pieces, including "Something for Ramon."

When I worked in Charles Mingus's band, I learned a lot from Mingus about counterpoint. I thought this would be a good vehicle to use in the bridge. The first 32 bars of the song have a Latin feel with a *basso ostinato*. In the 16-bar bridge, there's a samba feel. Then for the last 12 bars, the Latin feel returns. It's a very long structure, but for the solos on the live recording, the form was shortened to 16-16-12.

I would say the best way to interpret this song is with a "Spanish tinge."

Artist	Album	Label/Year
Kenny Barron	Live at Fat Tuesday's	Enja, 1988

Countin' on the Blues

"Countin' On The Blues" was conceived out of a need to write something in tribute to one of the great pianists and band leaders of the 20th century, Count Basie. When Count Basie passed on, I wrote a song for him that I didn't like. I kept changing it for about a year, and then finally one day it dawned on me that the composition shouldn't be totally written out. The pianist plays in the Count Basie style with the rhythm section as an introduction to the arrangement.

The piano introduction is a basic 12-bar blues, but when the horns enter with the melody, the band plays the arrangement. The soloists then improvise on the basic blues structure, utilizing the last 4 bars of the composition.

To interpret this song, the feeling should be in the Kansas City style, very loose but tight.

Artist	Album	Label/Year
John Stubblefield	Countin' on the Blues	Enja, 1987

Montauk

I used to fish in Montauk, Long Island, quite a bit in the early 1980s. One day while I was fishing, this melody came to me, and the chords were placed to it later.

The chords in "Montauk" are contemporary, and the movement has to do with the bass notes. The piece uses bitonal harmonies. The last 8 bars is a vamp that sets up the return to the beginning.

"Montauk" is a song that drummer Victor Lewis liked a lot when we recorded it. To interpret "Montauk," one should think in terms of the beauty of wide-open spaces.

Artist	Album	Label/Year
John Stubblefield	Countin' on the Blues	Enja, 1987

Serenade to the Motherland

"Serenade to the Motherland" came from a project record I did in 1986. My producer asked me to compose an album based on my explorations into African music and its effect on world music today. So I thought I would write a melody with an African feel to it. The song is a tribute to Africa and her musical riches.

This melody came out, a 16-bar melody in 6/4, which I answered by restating the melody, again for 16 bars. An 8-bar rhythmic release then follows.

This song should be played with a feeling of jubilation, not highlife, but in a very festive way.

Artist	Album	Label/Year
Olivier Gatto	What Is This Thing Called Love	—, 1993
John Stubblefield	Bushman Song	Enja, 1986

Bushman Song

"Bushman Song" grew out of that same effort, when my producer asked me to write songs with different kinds of feelings, but in the African tradition. For the melody, I used techniques that are employed by saxophonists today, coming from the mannerisms of John Coltrane, where one plays harmonics on the instrument with a certain fingering, getting a loping kind of sound. I wrote a 16-bar melody, answered it by repeating it, and kept building on it.

Mary Lou Williams always used to tell me, "John, you've got to write more interludes, more modulations in your music." So I decided to add an interlude in duple meter. The interlude should be played twice: the first time the last bar is in 2 beats, and the second time it's in 8 beats. Then one goes back for solos on the 32-bar form. The composition has been recorded by four different artists (including Mickey Tucker twice), and all have used the interlude.

We did two versions of "Bushman Song" on the first record: an acoustic version and a funky version with an electric bass. I've repainted the song now by adding different chords. Mickey Tucker and Louis Hayes have recorded the new version, while Teruo Nakamura used the original chords and gave the song a commercial feel with a hip hop beat.

I have a lot of fun playing "Bushman Song." It should be interpreted with spirit and fire.

Artist	Album	Label/Year
Mickey Tucker	176 Keys: Piano Thunder from Down Under	Sean Slug, 1992
Teruo Nakamura	Wind Smile	Cheetah, 1990
Mickey Tucker	Blues in Five Dimensions	Steeplechase, 1989
Louis Hayes	The Crawl	Candid, 1989
John Stubblefield	Bushman Song	Enja, 1986

Some Things Never Change

"Some Things Never Change" was also on that project album, *Bushman Song*. This was a song that came out all at once. I was having a blue day, and I went to the piano and played this chord. I remembered how Miles Davis would talk about how to make music dramatic. So I thought about how I could write a song that was the blues and add some kind of drama other than what is in a standard 12-bar blues format.

I struck this chord, and it came to me that if there was a bass line moving under the chord and the piano and drums had certain rhythmic responsibilities, I could add more suspense to the music. The drummer, who plays with brushes throughout the piece, also heightens the drama by picking up the sticks for the last 3 bars to bring out the 5/4 bar and take us back to the beginning.

The title "Some Things Never Change" refers to the fact that the blues is always there as the foundation. The song should be interpreted with the blues in mind, but not directly expressed.

Artist	Album	Label/Year
John Stubblefield	Bushman Song	Enja, 1986

You Know My Eyes

"You Know My Eyes" was composed in the summer of 1985. The song just came from one bar to the next. It was originally written in 6/4 time, and I changed it to 4/4. It has a basso ostinato for the first 8 bars, and then the bass is free for the last 8 bars. The chords are somewhat symmetrical in harmony, but they move all kinds of ways in order to express a feeling.

The best way to interpret "You Know My Eyes" is very tenderly, sensuously, and sensitively. Vincent Herring recorded the song on his album, "American Experience." Garnett Brown, one of my favorite trombonists, arrangers, and orchestrators, loves this composition.

Artist	Album	Label/Year
Vincent Herring	A Jazz Valentine	Music Masters, 1993
Vincent Herring	American Experience	Music Masters, 1990

Confessin'

What I had in mind in "Confessin'" was to write a song that would be a vehicle for an instrumentalist or singer to testify on. It was written initially in 4/4 time in 1981. When I got back to it in 1984, I realized that the time was not in 4 beats, but in 12, so I changed it to a compound quadruple meter.

The structure of "Confessin" is 11 bars in 12/4, with a one bar break in 4/4 in the 10th bar of the piece. The chords are very dark, and there is a basso ostinato going on under the polyrhythmic drums, with the melody floating on top of that.

Artist	Album	Label/Year
John Stubblefield	Confessin'	Soul Note, 1984

Dusk to Dawn

"Dusk to Dawn" was composed in two stages one night after I came home from work. Around dusk this melody came to me, and through the use of symmetrical harmonies and call and response, it grew into a 16-bar statement. The last 16 bars of this piece came just before dawn when I transposed the melody a fourth away from the original melody, using the same chords with slight changes.

After "Dusk to Dawn" was completed, I was commissioned to arrange it for an octet. For that performance, I added a shout chorus inspired by the style of the late Tadd Dameron.

This piece should swing in a contemporary manner.

Artist	Album	Label/Year
John Stubblefield	Confessin'	Soul Note, 1984

How I Think of You

"How I Think of You" was written in 1980 and recorded nine years later. I wrote the song to express my feelings in terms of what was going on in the final days of fusion. I also wanted to write a song that was very lyrical and flowing. The harmonies are symmetrical, and the release in the bridge is repeated throughout the piece. It has an AAB form of 32-12.

"How I Think of You" was recorded on Teruo Nakamura's record *Wind Smile*. This song has a contemporary Latin groove.

Artist	Album	Label/Year
Teruo Nakamura	Wind Smile	Cheetah, 1990

Midnight Over Memphis

"Midnight Over Memphis" is a song that grew out of a harmonic and rhythmic germ that I have heard and played many times in rhythm and blues and pop music. I wanted to write a song that would paint a portrait of my early musical life. It had to have the ingredients of gospel music and rhythm and blues.

At the time this piece was composed, I was traveling with Nat Adderley. "Midnight Over Memphis" was recorded by Hank Crawford and Nat Adderley around the same time. I've also recorded the song twice over the years.

To interpret this song, one might think in terms of being the lead singer in a gospel choir.

Artist	Album	Label/Year
John Stubblefield	Sophisticated Funk	Cheetah, 1990
John Stubblefield	Midnight Over Memphis	Nippon Columbia, 1978
Hank Crawford	Hank's Back	Kudu, 1977
Nat Adderley	Hummin'	Little David, 1976

Venus Eyes

I wrote "Venus Eyes" when I played in Roy Haynes's "Hip Ensemble." It was during the end of the disco period, and there were certain kinds of bass lines played then that utilized octave skips. I wrote 16 bars that drew on that sound and brought the piece to Roy's rehearsal. We played it, and Roy said, "That's it! John, you don't have to add no more to that."

The band loved it right away, and Roy Haynes recorded it about two years later. In 1978, I also recorded it with "Manhattan Blaze" for small orchestra and big band on Nippon Columbia Records.

Artist	Album	Label/Year
Roy Haynes	Vista Lite	Galaxy, 1979
Manhattan Blaze	Venus Eyes	Nippon Columbia, 1978

Amor Sonador

"Amor Sonador" came about one day while I was listening to the radio. I heard one chord of some song, went to the piano, and the whole composition came out. It's 32 bars in length. The chords, especially in the bridge, are influenced by the movie *Blood and Sand*. There's something about the music from that Rudolf Valentino movie that always stayed with me.

This piece should be played with a Latin feel.

Artist	Album	Label/Year
Chico Freeman	Pied Piper	Blackhawk, 1986
John Stubblefield	Midnight Sun	Sutra, 1980
Nat Adderley	Hummin'	Little David, 1976

Twelve for K.D.

"Twelve for K.D." kind of explains itself. When I came to New York, I had the opportunity to work with Kenny Dorham a couple of times, and I was with him at Minton's shortly before he died. I have always admired Kenny Dorham as one of the great trumpeters and composers in jazz. So I wrote this piece to acknowledge him on my first record.

For this composition I used the format of the minor 12-bar blues. The musicians who worked with Kenny Dorham said he would talk about writing codas "to bow out on." So I added a tag to "Twelve for K.D."

When I wrote the song, I played it for Jimmy Heath, who said, "That sounds something like K.D. would have written." We played it when I was touring with Nat Adderley.

The song should be interpreted as a minor blues, coming from the hard bop school.

Artist	Album	Label/Year
John Stubblefield	Prelude	Storyville, 1976

Little Prince

"Little Prince" was written in 1975 for my son. I was thinking about all the little kids in the world and what they would grow up to be. It is a musical portrait of John at three years of age.

The song is written in 3/4 meter. It's basically an African waltz. I chose this meter to write something for a child, because it seems very innocent. I wanted it to have a feeling of happiness, like a kid.

I have recorded "Little Prince" twice. The first time was on the album *Midnight Sun*, produced in 1975 and released in 1980. The second time was for Storyville Records in 1976. The best way to interpret the song is with an African waltz feel.

Artist	Album	Label/Year
John Stubblefield	Midnight Sun	Sutra, 1980
John Stubblefield	Prelude	Storyville, 1976

Discography

Artist	Year	Position	Title	Label
Jerry Gonzalez & Fort Apache Band	1995	S,C,A	Pensativo	Fantasy
Mingus Big Band	1995	S	Gunslingin' Bird	Dreyfus
Kenny Barron	1995	S	—	French/Verve
Jerry Gonzalez & Fort Apache Band	1994	S	Crossroads	Fantasy
Jean Paul Bourelly	1994	S	Blackadelic-Blu	DIW
John Stubblefield	1994	S,C,A	Morning Song	Enja
Larry Willis	1994	S	A Tribute to Someone	Audio Quest
McCoy Tyner	1994	S	Journey	Verve/Birdology
James Jabbo Ware	1994	S,C,A	Heritage	Soul Note
Mingus Big Band '93	1993	S	Nostalgia in Times Square	Dreyfus
Craig Harris	1993	S	F-Stop	Soul Note
Olivier Gatto*	1993	S,C,A	What Is This Thing Called Love	—
Franklin Kiermyer	1992	S	In the House of My Fathers	Konnex
Billy Hart	1992	S,C,A	Amethyst	Arabesque
Victor Lewis	1992	S	Family Portrait	Audio Quest

Artist	Year	Position	Title	Label
Teruo Nakamura	1992	S	Canary Island	Denon
Rory Stuart	1992	S	—	—
McCoy Tyner	1991	S	Turning Point	Verve/Birdology
Benny Powell	1991	S,C,A	You Gotta Say Yes	Inspire Productions
Kenny Barron	1991	S,C,A	Quickstep	Enja
Thurman Barker*	1990	S	—	—
John Stubblefield	1990	S,C,A	Sophisticated Funk	Cheetah
Teruo Nakamura	1990	S,C,A	Wind Smile	Cheetah
Norma Jean Wright & Raymond Jones	1990	S	Community	CBS
Abdullah Ibrahim	1989	S	African River	Enja
Pheeroan Aklaff	1989	S	Sonogram	MU Records
Louis Hayes	1989	S,C,A	The Crawl	Candid
Louis Hayes	1989	S	Una Max	Steeplechase
Kip Hanrahan	1988	S	Days & Nights of Blue Luck Invented	American Clave
Jerry Gonzalez & Fort Apache Band	1988	S	Obatala	Enja
Monteira/Young/ Holt& Friends	1988	S,C,A	Live at the Montreux Jazz Festival	WEA
Oliver Lake	1988	S	Other Side	Grammavision
Kenny Barron	1988	S,C,A	Live at Fat Tuesday's	Enja
Michael Carvin	1988	S,C,A	First Time	Muse
Julius Hemphill	1988	S	Julius Hemphill Big Band	Nonesuch
John Stubblefield	1987	S,C,A	Countin' on the Blues	Enja

Artist	Year	Position	Title	Label
John Stubblefield	1986	S,C,A	Bushman Song	Enja
Kenny Barron	1986	S	What If?	Enja
Harvie Swartz	1986	S	Smart Moves	Grammavision
Various Artists	1985	S	Lost in the Stars: The Music of Kurt Weill	A & M
John Stubblefield	1984	S,C,A	Confessin'	Soul Note
Kip Hanrahan	1983	S	Desire Develops an Edge	American Clave
Teo Macero	1983	S	Impressions of Charles Mingus	Palo Alto
Teo Macero	1983	S	Acoustical Suspension	Doctor Jazz
John Stubblefield	1982	S,A	School Daze Brothers Unique	Sutra
John Stubblefield*	1981	S,C,A	Peaceful Waters	Sutra
Harry Whitaker*	1980	S	The Afterlife	—
Kip Hanrahan	1980	S	Coup De Tete	American Clave
Kenny Barron	1980	S	Golden Lotus	Muse
Steve Gerassi*	1980	S	—	—
John Stubblefield	1979	S,C,A	Midnight over Memphis	Nippon Columbia
Manhattan Blaze	1978	S,C,A	Venus Eyes	Better Days
Sonny Phillips	1977	S	I Concentrate on You	Muse
Nat Adderley	1976	S,C,A	Hummin'	Little David
Nat Adderley	1976	S	Don't Look Back	Steeplechase
John Stubblefield	1976	S,C,A	Prelude	Storyville
Stanley Cowell	1976	S	Regeneration	Strata East

Artist	Year	Position	Title	Label
John Stubblefield**	1975	S,C,A	Midnight Sun	Sutra
M'tume	1975	S	Rebirth Cycle	Producers Circle
Henry Gross	1975	S	Release	Life Song
Lester Bowie	1975	S	Fast Lash	Muse
Reggie Lucas	1975	S	Survival Themes	Inner City
Miles Davis	1975	S	Get up with It	Columbia
McCoy Tyner	1974	S	Sama Layuca	Milestones
Roy Brooks	1974	S,C,A	Ethnic Expressions	Imhotep
Abdullah Ibrahim	1973	S	African Space Program	Enja
Anthony Braxton	1972	S	Town Hall	Trio
Maurice (Kalaparusha) McIntyre	1969	S	Humility in the Light of the Creator	Delmark
Joseph Jarman	1968	S	As If It Were the Season	Delmark
York Wilburn & The Thrillers	1963	S	Popeye	Devoice

*Unissued

**Released in 1980

Position Key:

S = Saxophonist

C = Composer

A = Arranger

Recorded Compositions

Composition	Artist	Title	Label/Year	Record #
Midnight Train	Jerry Gonzalez	Pensativo	Fantasy, 1995	—
Baby Man	Marian McPartland & Mary Lou Williams	Marian McPartland's Piano Jazz with Guest Mary Lou Williams	The Jazz Alliance, 1995	TJA 12019
Blues for the Moment King of Harts A Night in Lisbon Here and There	John Stubblefield	Morning Song	Enja, 1994	ENJ-8036 2
Cry of Hunger	James Jabbo Ware	Heritage	Soul Note, 1994	121259-2
Here and There Playroom Serenade to the Motherland	Olivier Gatto	What Is This Thing Called Love	—, 1993	—
You Know My Eyes	Vincent Herring	A Jazz Valentine: In The Mood For Love	Music Masters, 1993	65091
Baby Man	Andrew Cyrille	Jazz Methodology in Drum Music	Alchemy Pictures, 1993	Video #001
King of Harts	Billy Hart	Amethyst	Arabesque, 1992	AJ0105
Bushman Song	Mickey Tucker	176 Keys: Piano Thunder from Down Under	Sean Slug, 1992	DEX10013
Once Upon a Time Here and There	Kenny Barron	Quickstep	Enja, 1991	R279666

Composition	Artist	Title	Label/Year	Record #
Sophisticated Funk It's Time Midnight over Memphis One on One	John Stubblefield	Sophisticated Funk	Cheetah, 1990	CH03012
Bushman Song How I Think of You	Teruo Nakamura	Wind Smile	Cheetah, 1990	CH03011
You Know My Eyes	Vincent Herring	American Experience	Music Masters, 1990	5037-4-C
Bushman Song	Louis Hayes	The Crawl	Candid, 1989	CCD79045
Bushman Song	Mickey Tucker	Blues in Five Dimensions	Steeplechase, 1989	SCCD-31258
Something for Ramon High Priest*	Kenny Barron	Live at Fat Tuesday's	Enja, 1988	5071-49
M.R.	Michael Carvin	First Time	Muse, 1988	MC-5352
Countin' on the Blues Montauk The Wanderer	John Stubblefield	Countin' on the Blues	Enja, 1987	5051
Bushman Song Serenade to the Motherland Some Things Never Change Calypso Rose East Side West Side	John Stubblefield	Bushman Song	Enja, 1986	5015-12
Amor Sonador	Chico Freeman	Pied Piper	Blackhawk, 1986	BKH50801-CD
Confessin' Dusk to Dawn More Fun Spiral Dance	John Stubblefield	Confessin'	Soul Note, 1984	SN1095CD
Venus Eyes Peaceful Waters Dewey's Delight	John Stubblefield	Peaceful Waters	Sutra, 1981	Unissued
Song for One Little Prince Amor Sonador Free Spirits	John Stubblefield	Midnight Sun	Sutra, 1980	SUS 1004

Composition	Artist	Title	Label/Year	Record #
Eternal Star* How I Think of You*	Larry Smith	—	Cheetah, 1980	—
Baby Man	Andrew Cyrille	Special People	Soul Note, 1980	SN121012-1
Venus Eyes	Roy Haynes	Vista Lite	Galaxy, 1979	GXY5116
Venus Eyes	Manhattan Blaze	Venus Eyes	Nippon Columbia, 1978	YX-7589-ND
Midnight over Memphis Mimi Peaceful Waters*	John Stubblefield	Midnight over Memphis	Nippon Columbia, 1978	YX-7546-ND
Midnight over Memphis	Hank Crawford	Hank's Back	Kudu, 1977	KU-3351
Amor Sonador Midnight over Memphis	Nat Adderley	Hummin'	Little David, 1976	LD1012
Minor Impulse Little Prince Song for One Twelve for K.D.	John Stubblefield	Prelude	Storyville, 1976	SLP4011
Free Spirits Baby Man	Mary Lou Williams	Free Spirits	Steeplechase, 1975	SCS1043
Kera's Dance	The Awakening	Hear, Sense, and Feel	Black Jazz, 1972	BJQD/9

*Unissued

About the Author

Joyce **Stubblefield Pattillo** is the sister of John Stubblefield. She is a consultant with more than 30 years of experience in human resources. Her business, J Pat Consulting, is dedicated to motivating management to enhance their leadership skills and build stronger teams. J Pat Consulting is sought after to design company initiatives, facilitate focus groups, customize training, and conduct and analyze employee surveys. She founded the firm with motivation from John, who provided mentorship, books, and his ongoing words of encouragement—"Joyce you can do this." Writing this book was far off the grid from what Joyce does professionally; however, it remained in her heart for many years. With gracious support and encouragement, it is now a reality. Joyce resides in Little Rock, Arkansas.